Chaldean Numerology
An Ancient Map for Modern Times

by

Leeya Brooke Thompson

TENACITY PRESS

Copyright © 1999 by Leeya Brooke Thompson

TENACITY PRESS
1-800-738-6721

ISBN 1-892193-10-8
CIP 99-70900

Cover design by
GeoGraphics
Rixanne Wehren
PO Box 340, Albion, CA 95410
707-937-2709

Printed by
Morris Publishing
Kearney, NE 68847
1-800-650-7888

1 2 3 4 5 6 7 8 9

To Lily

We shared a Life Path and a Teacher
What a trip we've been on!

TABLE OF CONTENTS

Foreword

It's Thanksgiving today. As I sit at my computer with rain falling from the first winter storm outside my window, I am filled with gratitude for a life filled with adventure, family, friendships and the map of numerology which has been an important guide to me for over 35 years.

Would I have gone as bravely through this life of mine without the map? I believe I can answer that with a convincing *no*. The clarity and understanding I received from my own map of numerology provided clues and significance to help me through the unpleasant experiences that life occasionally doled out to me. And by discerning the meaning and the lesson behind the experiences, I learned to accept and be more faithful to my path.

Beyond guiding my own steps, having the ability to chart out this map for other people allowed me precious glimpses into the diverse ways and strategies life offers us. We may be One but we are not the same! Learning to respect our differences would take us a long way towards achieving world peace.

For many years the map of numerology I used followed the instructions given in the popular Western system, sometimes called the Pythagorean method. I became increasingly skeptical of the information I received even though the analysis of the number patterns was exceedingly helpful. In many respects, I felt the popular study of numerology had let me down and I had serious questions about it as a reliable source of information to explain our inner self and outer experiences.

Five years ago I was introduced to the Chaldean system of numerology. Curious as to what changes it would make in my chart, I constructed charts for myself and members of my family. I was astonished with the accuracy of the information I received. Pieces of the puzzle that had not fit before, using the Pythagorean system, all of a sudden found their place, creating a picture of me and my family which I knew in my heart was accurate. I then proceeded to construct and interpret charts for others, some people I knew who had faithfully pursued self-knowledge over the years, and some people whom I did not know at all. Without exception their feedback gave me the assurance that the Chaldean approach to numerology offered much valuable information.

The primary difference between the Chaldean system and Western Pythagorean numerology is in the assignment of different numerical values to a few of the letters. These changes are necessitated by certain sound vibrations associated with these letters. Let me explain: there is a scientific rationale, correlating sound vibration with organic patterns, which gives clues as to how and why a subject as seemingly esoteric as numerology could work at all. Yet, alas, we do not have the benefit of having had the proof performed with modern, scientific technology, so we are left with an imperfect system with hopes that someone, someday, will take this as a subject of research and provide us with truly accurate information.

But even an imperfect system for self knowledge, which introduces us to an immortal part of ourselves—the Self that makes choices and takes responsibility to use our misguided or ignorant actions as source material for life lessons—is preferable to continuing to deny this greater reality of who we are. The earth has seriously been compromised because of the materialistic view that we could discount the presence of invisible spirit within physical life. We know better now, and with the knowledge that consciousness pervades all matter and that we live on a sentient earth, hopefully we will begin to make different choices than the ones we made in the past.

In the beginning of my study of numerology I had a teacher, read many books and eventually internalized my own understanding of the numbers and the key positions of the numerology map. In this book I will share my understanding of these vibrational patterns in relation to a person's life.

In Section I there is a brief discussion about this more ancient approach. In-depth meditations to assist in the understanding of the number patterns are given in Section II. Section III provides step by step instructions on setting up a chart to illuminate the complete picture offered by numerology before interpreting any one position. In Section IV the name is analyzed to shed light on the characteristics of the person who is walking the journey. Section V delineates the nature of the journey itself as disclosed by the birth date. Section VI discusses the challenges confronting the Journeyer. Section VII defines the Power Goal one is moving towards and the yearly cycles one passes through towards that Goal. Section VIII offers examples of how to interpret the chart as a whole and integrate it so that one sees, not simplistic bits and pieces of a person, but the rich complexity of the whole person. Section IX briefly discusses how to compare charts in order to have a deeper understanding of the purpose and meaning of one's' relationships.

I wish to acknowledge Marie Shaw, my first teacher, who spent hours going over my chart with me, showing me how to lay it out so that it could be read clearly–truly a great gift. Also for the helpful information in the books of Juno Jordan and those of many other numerologists, especially W. Mykian who introduced me to the Chaldean System. However, more than reading any book, the opportunity to observe the functioning of the numbers in my own life as well as my clients, and the hours spent with my friends Barbara Stanley and Lily Kyle pondering the meaning of the numbers, have been my greatest teachers once the formal foundation of numerology had been laid. I could not have taken the step of publishing this book without the enormous help and encouragement of Hal Bennett and Susan Sparrow who gave unstintingly of their time and friendship and belief in my work.

Leeya Brooke Thompson
November 26, 1998

I

BASICS: THE MAP

Introduction

How many times have you heard someone ask in a state of confusion and pain, who am I and why am I here? These must be the most important questions we can ever ask ourselves. In my own life when I find myself in a state of chaos, or even mild confusion, these questions or something very similar to them, present themselves again and again until I become quiet and remember the answers. The world has a way of pressing in on us, luring us onto paths not necessarily in keeping with our own unique purpose. Finding our way back to ourselves can be a challenge, yet once we arrive, how good it is to be home!

If you have lost your way, or feel you never had it in the first place, take heart. In the pages ahead we will be exploring a map of consciousness that can provide direction and meaning for you personally. The oldest map we know of, reaching back before recorded history, is the belief that numbers have a sacred meaning which can be applied to our lives and the world around us. We call this the map of numerology.

Assigning sacred meaning to numbers was discredited with the advent of material science which promised to unlock all the secrets of the universe by rational and observable means. A schism developed between spirit on the one hand and physical matter on the other. The world we live in today is a result of that split. To regain a healthy life and planet, this split must be healed.

Fortunately, a growing number of free-thinking scientists are rediscovering the inner meanings of numbers and the means by which vibration creates geometrical and organic forms. The sacred wisdom of numbers, to my knowledge, has not yet been recovered, but is on its way to being so. In the meantime we have numerological systems passed down to us from antiquity, perhaps damaged and incomplete, yet still capable of shedding light upon our lives. Through this light we attempt to interpret what we see. The artful interpretation of a life through an understanding of numbers is what we strive to achieve in our study and application of numerology.

Historical Background for Numerology

Numerology, the science of numbers, is one of the oldest maps of consciousness around. It has been called upon to help us understand our lives perhaps since the beginning of recorded history.

Pythagoras, considered the Father of modern numerology, lived in Asia Minor 2,500 years ago. As a young man he followed his desire to acquire knowledge and ventured out into the known world to gather in what the great minds had passed down through the mystery schools of Egypt, Chalde, Judea and India. By the time he was 60 years old, he had amassed a vast fund of information, including mathematics, astronomy, physics and philosophy. These subjects became the basis of study for a school he founded for a religious brotherhood.

Discerning the nature of sound vibrations, Pythagoras understood the importance of numbers to science. More than just digits for counting or mathematical equations, numbers were symbols providing a language to communicate the knowledge of the various vibrational patterns constituting nature. However, much of Pythagoras' teachings were lost when he fell from favor towards the end of his life and his papers were destroyed. One of his students, in an attempt to recreate the study of numbers, set up a system which has come down through the ages to the present day. He assigned numbers to the letters of the alphabet sequentially, rather than relating the number symbol to the sound vibration, the mechanism that creates the pattern. There is no indication that Pythagoras had ever turned away from the knowledge of sound vibration with the correspondent number as taught by his Chaldean teachers. So his has been a damaged system, sorely missing the very element which made it a science. Indeed, the modern alphabet we use in the Western world was not even in existence 2,500 years ago. So how could a science of sound vibration known as numerology be based on a system assigning numbers to sequential letters in *our* alphabet?

In every other respect, such as the positions on the chart, Chaldean and Pythagorean (Western) Numerology are identical. If you have used numerology in the past, the transition from the Western to the Chaldean system will be made with ease.

Maps of Consciousness

Most of us love a good story. One of our favorites is the journey story. A quest or a restlessness with the status quo, motivates a hero or heroine to begin an arduous and dangerous journey. Along the way s/he encounters challenges and adversaries, but also finds companions and allies with whom to share the dangers and pleasures of the road, celebrate victories, mourn defeat, and finally, for the happy ending, arrive at the hoped for goal.

Humanity has heard thousands of variations of this story over thousands of years, yet it always seems fresh and new. Each story belongs to us, it is our own story. We are the Journeyer and as we travel down our road, we hope in our secret heart that we, too, will achieve our happy goal.

A journey, to be successful and not end up going in circles, profits by having a map at hand to keep the Journeyer moving confidently toward the goal and to remind him where he is going. Maps of consciousness are offered by religions, psychological methodologies, folk wisdom and metaphysics. Perhaps you have heard of some of these metaphysical maps: Astrology, I-Ching, Runes, Tarot. Each one of them presents insights about ourselves and the world we live in, colored by its own unique perception and the culture which developed the map.

Numerology is also one of these maps of consciousness. Not only is the route clearly laid out as to how best to proceed, but you, the traveler on your heroic journey, are given information about the strengths you bring with you and the weaknesses which you need to confront and balance out before your goal can be reached. You are shown the pitfalls you fell into the last time you attempted this journey, and you find clues for rectifying them this time. And if you have chosen a companion to accompany you, you can discover why you are together and what you might accomplish in your relationship.

What journey will you take and what will be your attitude as you take it? Each trip is uniquely personal. By including ten major positions in a numerology chart, the odds of another person having an identical chart to yours are one million to one. Your specific journey may be down a road many others have gone; however, no one will experience it exactly as you do, nor bring to it the opportunities for growth which you bring. As you travel your road, it changes you and you change it.

Thoughts For The Road

- You are never alone on your life journey. Call it your soul, your angel, your higher self, or whatever you will, you have a constant companion with you, helping you arrive at your ultimate goal. In this book, I call it the soul. You may have forgotten this companion as you grew up, conforming to a disbelieving culture, but this awareness can be regained as you start to pay attention to the forces at work in your life through your numerological map of consciousness.

- I am constantly reminded of the awesome beauty of cosmic design when I sit down and interactively go through a querent's chart. To see how balance and completeness is choreographed by the soul makes numerology an ever fresh experience.

- No parent with more than one child can believe the baby is born as a blank slate. Each one of us arrives already formed with a personality and desires.

5

- We can be so much more contented with our lives if we walk down our own road instead of one someone else has decided we should take. There is a sense of rightness when we are expressing our deepest desires and fulfilling our life's purpose. Our chart can provide the bones of awareness, but it is our own inner knowing and outer expression which flesh out the chart. Rather than being a passive spectator of your chart, expecting the consultant to tell your fortune, wrestle with the information offered by the number patterns, challenge them, dig up your own experiences, thoughts and emotions and compare them to what your chart indicates. Let your chart prime the pump that allows your own truth to reveal itself. It may be you end up throwing your chart out with an exclamation of rubbish, but in the process, you've come to a clearer understanding of yourself. That's what is important!

- In *The Celestine Prophesy* James Redfield made the concept of synchronicity—the phenomenon of acausal relationships—something we can all understand. The skeptic may say, "My name is a mistake, so how could the numbers in my name mean anything to me?" If answering the skeptic with the concept that the incarnating soul made sure it had its proper name doesn't convince him or her, then we can bring in the principle of synchronicity: We don't know why you were given the name you have, but synchronistically it's perfect. It gives you the vibrational patterns you need to successfully walk your Life Path!

- When you begin to understand the symbolic language of numbers describing the vibrational patterns, you begin to develop an appreciation for how these patterns interact with each other, and why the soul would have chosen certain difficult interactions in order to strengthen weak attributes in yourself and lead you to a higher balance of energies and compassion. I think of the soul as having a much broader perspective than held by our personality self. It has the ability to see time laid out as a whole, with past-present-future all of one piece, and the probable consequences of actions we have taken or will take. Therefore, experiences that may seem unpleasant to you in the present could be viewed by your soul as necessary for your greater happiness and fulfillment.

- One of the mistaken ideas about numbers is that some numbers are good and some bad, some lucky and some unlucky. There is no such thing as good or bad, lucky or unlucky, except insofar as the energy people give to the number or the superstition they may feel about that number. The number is a symbol for a universal pattern as mentioned above. What you do with that pattern is what determines whether the expression of it is good or bad, lucky or unlucky. The pattern in itself is neutral. It may be that you do not like the pattern in front of you, since it is in the nature of humans to resist change, the unknown, or a challenge; however, if your number can be seen as representing the pattern that must be mastered in order to move forward on the journey, then it becomes less a disagreeable experience to be avoided and more one to be embraced with gratitude.

Understanding The Patterns

Numerology is based on single-digit numbers, that is, only the numbers from 1 to 9. In most systems, you have to either refer back to a chart of attributes or memorize the patterns that each one of the numbers symbolizes. However, there is an easier way to remember them. Think of the numbers from 1 to 9 telling a story. When viewed in this way they are not only easier to remember, they also remind us that they are associated with universal themes in all of human life. To best understand this, let's make a story about the life of a pioneer, based on the nine numbers.

Pattern 1 Individuality - Self - Masculine

Before anything can be manifested in the physical dimension, there first has to be an awareness on the part of our hypothetical pioneer of a continent or potentiality out there to be explored. He, for it is the masculine drive in this pattern, desires to achieve this new territory and to conquer the uncharted wilderness. This is not a fearful person clinging to the known reality, but one with self confidence and courage. It is his sense of himself, a dominant, individualistic nature, that allows him to break out of the old boundaries and face the challenges of the unknown. He goes out alone, finds the setting and eventually desires companionship.

Pattern 2 - Duality - The Feminine

He finds a wife, a companion and partner with whom he can share his new land and learns cooperation and awareness of other people. She may find it difficult to leave the comfort of the old, yet his strength allows her to embrace this new experience where she bridges the perspective of the old and that of the new. Unlike her husband, whose one-focused determination brought him through dangers to the new land, she notices everything along the way. She brings sensitivity, understanding and comfort to him, stabilizing his restless drive into the new. In the duality of their relationship they can sense the dimensions and polarities of experience confronting them. She finds security in the peace she strives to maintain in her relationship with her sometimes aggressive and domineering husband, and the need to complete their relationship in a creative outpouring becomes uppermost.

Pattern 3 - Emergence - The Child

Together the husband and wife bring forth a child. Joy comes into their lives as they experience the spontaneous and imaginative self-expression of their child. The child bubbles over with words and sounds and prodigiously starts all those wonderful projects and pieces of art children seem capable of bringing into the world. Signs of creativity clutter the environment as the child is more interested in expression and not at all interested in finishing or cleaning up after itself. Nevertheless, the family unit feels complete as the companionship of husband and wife expands to include the child or children and all their friends. Yet now a place needs to be built to contain this family unit.

Pattern 4 - Structure - Foundation Building

Attention is now brought into focus with the construction of the foundation to contain this family. Perseverance, endurance, patience, hard work and loyalty are called for in this pattern of foundation building. Fortunately, our pioneer family has these qualities and wishes to build strongly for the future. They may have to clear a spot in the wilderness, pick through rock to dig their foundation trenches, cut down trees, mold adobe bricks, but they enjoy the hard, physical labor. This pattern represents the salt of the earth, the loyal, conservative, tried and true member of any organization. Once the foundation work has been completed, the desire is to expand, to move out of the nitty gritty, to be a bit less hard working and explore the world as in Pattern 5.

Pattern 5 - Freedom - Gathering Experience - Change

And what a world it is! The senses are overwhelmed with smells, sights, sounds, textures, ideas, new people and places. This pattern is charged with curiosity about everything exciting, different, unusual, and sensual. There is a drive to take it all in, to absorb, to mingle, to travel, to feel, to taste the world. This is truly the pattern of humanity, the rolling stone which gathers no moss but lots of polish! Freedom burns in the heart of this pattern, freedom to experience the world. However, there comes a time when a sense of responsibility to the family at home, and a desire for stability and roots becomes even more important than the gypsy life.

Pattern 6 - Responsibility - Service

The Pioneer, who has now become the Journeyer, for she is now a sophisticated and worldly person, returns to the foundations of her home with all the knowledge, experience and acquisitions gathered in her travels. The home and family benefit from the culture and beauty discovered out there and what had been rather bare walls before, now takes on a glow of culture and refinement. The children are nurtured and taught, their development in the arts is encouraged. The Journeyer takes pleasure in serving the family, community, classroom and is a patron of the arts. A higher level of love is cultivated in companionship and family life. Yet even this happy situation grows stale to the restless soul which is never willing to stagnate in the status quo and, just as the outer world has been explored, the focus now turns to an inward search.

Pattern 7 - Wisdom - Detachment

The Journeyer is now at that place in life where he can step back from the emotions and outer distractions in order to probe more deeply into the inner workings of nature. By being detached, he can discover more clearly what is true, what is at the core of things and the cause of life. A desire to know what makes things tick motivates a scientific or metaphysical exploration of the universe. No longer is the Journeyer interested in mingling and social life, but rather wishes the peace and perfection of the Halls of Learning, the mountain top, the retreat center. Meditation, contemplation, pure research, the inspiration of nature and music, the lofty and intense discussion with colleagues, the joy of exposure to Truth, are the pursuits of this pattern. The inner life is explored and mastered and a yearning for outer expression begins to dominate the Journeyer.

Pattern 8 - Mastery - Power

The Journeyer has become a person of mastery over the physical and the non-physical worlds. She has reached a pinnacle of experience from which she can view the entire field of opportunity. Now she must make some important decisions regarding what she wants to keep and preserve, what she desires to accomplish on a scale far grander than anything she has yet achieved. The education and experiences she acquired in her formative years now determines how successfully she will administer and direct the energy of people and finance. This is her destiny and birthright and the drive to administer will be there, happily or with difficulty. With the 8 pattern she is in a position to make astute choices and judgments, to prioritize tasks, and to direct organizations. She works with power. Much is demanded of the Journeyer and, if she has done her homework, she enjoys exercising her power. Yet even power can become tiresome on the Soul's long journey through life, and there comes a time when she yearns to move beyond her personal life and limitations and unite with something much bigger, much more transcendent, perhaps with the Universal Ocean of life itself, to become one with God.

Pattern 9 - Universality - Transcendence

This is the pattern which moves beyond the personal into a transpersonal awareness. The Journeyer, so far removed from the individualism found in the 1 Pattern, feels and experiences the drama of all life. In sensing the pain, the joy, the highs and lows of others, he develops compassion and empathy capable of forgiving all trespasses for he comprehends on a gut level what motivates others and recognizes himself and his own shortcomings. No longer feeling separate or needing power for himself, he only desires to melt in with others. He finds artistic expression, especially drama, as a way to reach into the hearts and souls of others and to touch them, to inspire and to heal. But there comes a time when a need arises to rediscover and affirm his own individuality. Withdrawing from the collective mentality, he sets his sights on the unknown, the mystery, becoming a pioneer once again. The spiral continues.

Further Examination of the Number Patterns

In the story above, we see the story progression of a pioneer, moving from: 1–a solo existence, through 2–mating, 3–parenting, 4–building, 5–changing, 6–serving, 7–detaching, 8–gaining mastery, and finally 9–transcending. Here is another story line showing how the numbers might be applied to farming or gardening:

Pattern 1   Seeds are planted - a *new beginning.*

Pattern 2   We *nurture* their germination by watering and fertilizing them.

Pattern 3   They *emerge* from the soil and we rejoice in their sprouting.

Pattern 4   We *tend* our crop diligently, watering, weeding, cultivating, fertilizing.

Pattern 5   We *expand* our gardening knowledge by attending gardening classes. We talk with others about our plants, finding ways to harvest, preserve, and utilize them to their fullest.

Pattern 6   We return to our garden and *responsibly* implement our increased knowledge of

13

horticulture, bringing our crop along to its greatest fulfillment.

Pattern 7   We've become engrossed, with delight, in our plants and want to *know* more about their inner process of growth, also the biology of the insects which help or harm them. We study while our crop is coming to fruition.

Pattern 8   Our crop is ready to be *harvested*. We call in workers to help us pick, separate the wheat from the chaff and to preserve the crop. We pay our workers their dues. We sell some of our produce to cover costs and invest in future projects.

Pattern 9   Our gardening *cycle has ended*. We've done well with our harvest and now clean up our fields to prepare for next year's crop. Because we know what it's like not to have food, we share our abundance with others.

II

UNCOVERING THE NUMBER PATTERNS

Introduction

Until we have met a person and experienced the impact of their physical reality, that person is somewhat of an abstraction, a name, perhaps a voice, even though we may have statistics of their age, the kind of work they are in, their address and phone number. This is all helpful information to flesh out the general facts about a person. However it is only when we stand opposite that person, breathe in their smell, see the colors of their eyes, hear the subtle tones of their voice, feel the press of their hand, sense the energy which radiates from them and observe their body posture, that we receive a deeper knowledge of who this person is and how we connect with him or her.

This section will give you all the information about the primary number patterns allowing you to construct the living reality of each pattern in your own imagination. Read the attributes and description of each pattern, then put the book down, close your eyes, and imagine someone in your own experience who expresses this pattern. Perhaps this is someone you know well, a friend, sister, parent, teacher. See them in a new way with your new information.

Obviously, no person is a pure number pattern, but sometimes a pattern can be so striking that seeing how your acquaintance uses the pattern can broaden your understanding of them. If you don't know a person who expresses one of the patterns, then make one up. Or you might even think about a person from history or from a novel you've read. Give your imaginary person color, voice, smell, emotions. Picture them doing something and watch how they do it in your mind. What is their body language like, the expressions they use, how do they laugh, eat, sleep? In your journal, describe or glue in pictures of people or things which seem to illustrate each respective   pattern for you, and your own meditative understanding of that pattern. This is your opportunity to make the information on the number patterns belong to you.

When you learn to construct your own chart further on in this book, there may be number patterns in positions on your chart which may feel strange or unfamiliar to you. Return to this section on Uncovering the Number Patterns and look up that number.   Particularly study the negative and denial expressions of the number. Are you perhaps acting out of the negative polarity of the pattern?   If so, work with the Affirmations which have been offered as a means of repolarizing your pattern from the negative to the positive side.

Once again, by using your powers of visualization, create an image of yourself expressing the pattern in a positive way. Every evening before going to sleep, review this positive image and make a mental, or even a physical note in your journal, of when you were able to express this pattern in a constructive way. Acknowledge your accomplishments in some tangible way such as rewarding yourself, giving yourself a pat on the back, a medal of achievement, or some concrete way that reminds you daily that you can be strong where you were weak before, you can find ways to cooperate when you had only insisted on your own way before. Working with the positive side of your number pattern will open floodgates of new energy and opportunity.

Once you have grasped the differences in the number patterns, you will be able to see people not as clones or projections of yourself but as each one expressing his or her life in a unique way. This is not only incredibly liberating for you, but moves you into a non-judgmental space, for why should other people respond exactly as you would? We each have our own paths and innate capacities to fulfill and Spirit has given us numerous ways to do this.

Internalize the number patterns and you will have mastered the keys of numerology. With this expertise, the charts you work on will easily fall into place and your ability to construct a chart and see how the various patterns interact with each other, will move out of the realm of the mysterious and arcane and into the understandable.

1

Image	EXPLORER/INVENTOR
Desire	TO PIONEER AND CREATE A NEW WAY
Pattern	CONCEPTION - INDIVIDUALITY

Positive Expression
masculine
mentally creative
courageous
ambitious
organizer
leader
pioneer
individualist
self confident
focused
original
competitive
positive
inventive
self-reliance
explorer
will power
robust
resourceful

Negative Expression
selfish
domineering
arrogant
aggressive
impulsive
obstinate
self-centered
boastful
bossy

Denial Expression
dependent
helpless
lazy--procrastinates
fearful
unwilling to take a stand
weak
submissive
stubborn

A Positive Vision For 1

One is the quality of Mind, capable of moving boldly into the unknown to seek out or invent new possibilities for all. A leader, the **1** is strong, independent, resourceful, and courageous. The **1,** secure in the knowledge of what he wants, goes after it with focused intent, and woe be unto the person who stands in his way!

New projects are initiated by the **1** vibration. An original thinker, others look to the **1** for fresh solutions. The **1** blazes the trail and leads the way. Others lean on the **1,** a relationship it enjoys and cultivates. Strong, masculine, dominant, and sometimes domineering, a **1**'s presence can never be ignored.

Where weaker and more thoughtful vibrations might hesitate, the courage or rashness of a **1** dares to break through limiting barriers, whether in self-expression, in business, social dealings, or in the exploration of space.

AFFIRMATIONS FOR 1

*I have the courage to face the unknown
and fulfill my life.*

*I can be strong for others and open doors
to new possibilities.*

*I have the self confidence to create a better world
for myself and others.*

I can assert my full individuality.

2

Image   DIPLOMAT - COOPERATION

Desire   PEACE - PARTNERSHIP - BALANCE

Pattern   GESTATION - DUALITY

Positive Expression
feminine
balance
diplomatic
adaptable
rhythmic
gentle
harmonious
receptive
aware of details
considerate
sensitive
friendly
companionship
tactful
peacemaker
kind
thoughtful
psychic ability
considerate
cooperative
reflective

Negative Expression
dependent
self-pity
too emotional
too sensitive
meddling
arbitrary
careless
strident
tactless
extremist
dishonest
overlooks detail
creates divisiveness
resentful
unforgiving

Denial Expression
insensitive/rude
overly concerned
  about detail
faultfinding
vacillating

A Positive Vision For 2

As a symbol of duality—the universe of opposites in which we live—the **2** stands alongside the **1**, offering a perspective of balance to **1**s narrow point of view. The **2** individual is able to see both sides of the equation through a fine discernment of detail, often beyond conscious awareness.

The **2**s highly tuned emotional nature can often grasp the subtleties of human interaction where the intellect alone is lost. Therefore the **2** is able to bridge the chasm of misunderstanding and become a peacemaker. Indeed, the **2** desires peace and harmony in all relationships and can be in danger of self denial or meddling in order to bring about this desired condition.

A **2** energy, in a positive mode, is the perfect partner and companion, smoothing the way with a desire for mutual cooperation. The **2** adapts easily to situations where a more rigid or focused vibration is unable to go.

AFFIRMATIONS FOR 2

*I find the truth in both sides of an argument
and create bridges of understanding.*

*I can cooperate with others while
remaining true to myself.*

*I find my point of balance and peace within myself
and bring these qualities into my relationships.*

3

Image	**JOYOUS CHILD**
Desire	**JOY -- SELF EXPRESSION**
Pattern	**EMERGENCE -- MANIFESTATION**

Positive Expression
social awareness
creative self-expression
artistic talent
charming
witty
happy
cheerful
spontaneous
talent for words
optimism
enthusiasm
affectionate
good conversationalist
loves a good time
manifestor
adaptable
sensitive

Negative Expression
dilettante
too easy going
trivial
superficial
extravagant
lack of concentration
impractical
vain
prone to exaggeration
childish
scatters energy

Denial Expression
critical
moody
too sensitive
gossipy
withholding
gloomy
pessimistic

A Positive Vision For 3

Just as we all rejoice at the sight of the first shoots of flowers and buds on a tree in the Springtime, so is there a joyous burst of creative energy and expression in the number **3**. A mystic power resides in **3**—the Triune Deity, the 3 Fates, past/present/future, the point of synthesis that reconciles opposing views.

3 is a number of manifestation. What was conceived in **1** and nurtured in **2** now emerges into the physical world for all to witness. The emergence is imaginative, expressive and spontaneous. Words in speech and song are avenues of **3** expression.

3 symbolizes the inner child, often called the Divine Child. When **3** figures strongly in a chart, the individual is one who can see the world with new eyes, learns quickly, is adaptable and always ready to play. The **3** loves companionship and is a friend who can delight and entertain others with imagination and the ability to fantasize.

AFFIRMATIONS FOR 3

A loving Universe supports my Inner Child
and I become the artist I know is inside myself.

I express myself freely and joyously.

I love my ability to play --
to be spontaneous and expressive.

Communicating with others is easy and enjoyable.

23

4

Image	**HARD WORKER**
Desire	**TO BUILD & WORK -- INTEGRITY**
Pattern	**CONTAINMENT -FOUNDATION BUILDING**

Positive Expression
structure
practical
persevering
dependable
integrity
hard worker
organization
concentration
routine
endurance
loyal
truthful
builder
containment
conserving
tenacious
pragmatic
industrious

Negative Expression
dull
drudgery
unimaginative
short sighted
fixed
unadaptable
resistance
stubborn
nose to grind
 stone
obstinate
fixed–unadaptable
compulsive in work

Denial Expression
impractical
lazy
impatient
dishonest
scattered

A Positive Vision For 4

The **4** experiences deep satisfaction in physical labor. What can be work for other number patterns is considered play by the **4**. The opportunity to organize and build something of substance, something that will benefit the practical aspects of life motivates the **4** to heroic efforts.

4s are the salt of the earth, pillars of dependability in a family or community, those who are not afraid to leap into hard work and create a home, a garden, a piece of furniture, a structurally sound building. They persevere and endure where other numbers fall to the wayside or don't wish to dirty their fingernails.

There is a solid presence, integrity and loyalty in a strong, positive **4**. Although not a visionary, the **4** has the quality that brings into reality the visions of others through hard, persistent effort. The **4** will single-mindedly move towards the chosen goal, focus on the task, and feels rewarded when the job is accomplished.

AFFIRMATIONS FOR 4

*I find my greatest joy in working
intelligently and willingly.*

*I can be depended upon to persevere
until the job is done.*

*My efforts create order out of chaos,
both for myself and others.*

5

Image	**ADVENTURER ON THE OPEN ROAD**
Desire	**EXPERIENCE – CURIOSITY – FREEDOM**
Pattern	**CHANGE**

Positive Expression
versatility
adaptability
excitement
freedom
curiosity
exploration
energetic
charismatic
communicator
active
change
variety
adventurer
articulate
quick
savvy
sensual

Negative Expression
restless
irresponsible
rolling stone
slippery
procrastinator
scatters energy
philanderer
dilettante
glib
ignores laws
addictions

Denial Expression
fearful of change
sexual confusion
uncertain
unable to learn from
    experience

A Positive Vision for 5

Five is considered the number of humanity for it is by entering into the spirit of adventure and indulging in the satisfaction of our curiosity that we learn the fullness of the world in which we live.

A restlessness to explore, to examine the diversities of people, cultures, ideas and to learn from all the senses is the opportunity and the challenge of the **5**. Where the **4** is content to remain within the confines of space and status quo, **5** wants to burst out of all constraints and be free to *be*, to *do*, to *taste*, to *touch*.

And all this experiencing creates excitement, for the **5** has tales to tell and adventures to share. A positive **5** will be the life of a party, a salesperson without peer, being an eloquent, persuasive talker and unconcerned with the future. For when the future arrives, the **5** will be long gone - off on another adventure!

AFFIRMATIONS FOR 5

I am adaptable to new situations,
for change is my opportunity for progress.

All my senses are open to receive
the truth and beauty in this Earth.

I am charged with exhilaration and delight
with the experiences of everything around me.

27

6

Image	**PATRON OF THE ARTS**
Desire	**SERVICE – RELATIONSHIP**
Pattern	**RESPONSIBILITY – SERVICE**

Positive Expression
friendship
love
creative self-expression
culture
conventional
   understanding
broad-minded
sympathetic
create stability
selfless
humanitarian
moral
idealist
artistic
harmonious
nurturing
protective
warm & cozy

Negative Expression
controlling/possessive
martyr
compulsive
judgmental
too emotional
resentful
interfering
over-protective/worrier
narrow minded
bigot/opinionated
fanatic
jealous

Denial Expression
irresponsible
unable to express love and
   friendship
careless
indolent

A Positive Vision For 6

Having learned the ways of the world in **5**, the **6** now takes the responsibility for creating an environment of beauty and harmony. Those who experience this environment will be nurtured, healed, taught, and parented. The **6** finds joy in service, in uplifting others towards a higher, finer life, and in nurturing relationships.

Often considered the number of love and marriage, the **6** can also find these needs met in ministering to others as teacher, counselor and minister. Expression through the arts is natural for a **6** who loves to dance, to paint, to write poetry, to play a musical instrument. And if life denies opportunities for personal artistic expression, the **6** will be a great patron of the arts and appreciate the accomplishments of others.

The **6** is idealistic, envisioning a kinder, better world, seeing the highest of what another can be, wishing to build a society where art and culture can nurture the souls of its citizens. **6s** can sacrifice themselves for others and will do so willingly and lovingly as a parent will lay down his or her own life for their child.

AFFIRMATIONS FOR 6

I am able to respond appropriately
and intelligently to whomever I encounter.

I serve others without strings attached
and with a generous heart.

My love for others allows them
to fulfill their highest potential.

7

Image	TRUTH SEEKER/SCIENTIST
Desire	TO KNOW TRUTH — ANALYSIS
Pattern	WISDOM — DETACHMENT

Positive Expression
truthfulness
analysis
technical ability
scientific investigation
specialized
desire to understand
   fundamentals
desires proof
thinker/scholar
love of facts
intuitive
perfection
faith
wise
teacher
meditation
contemplative
sensitive

Negative Expression
anti-social
aloof
sarcastic
too analytical
harshly critical
eccentric
hard to understand
suppress feelings
perfectionism
nit-picking/fault
   finding
intellectual conceit

Denial Expression
skeptical/cynical
cold
body-mind split
inferiority complex
suppressive
secretive

A Positive Vision For 7

Seven withdraws from the bustle of ordinary life in order to enter into Life at deeper levels. A desire to know core meanings motivates the 7 to engage mind and intuition fully. Probing, examining, analyzing, contemplating, the 7 is the scholar, the scientist, the metaphysician, the priest(ess) who uncovers new frontiers in the world within and the deeper answers to life's most pressing concerns.

Finding these deeper answers strengthens faith in a Higher Intelligence, in purpose and meaning and moves the Seeker away from fear and into a position of strength with what is deeply perceived and known.

The beauty of nature and the harmony of fine music soothe and heal the sensitive soul of 7 who finds the noise of crowds and the rat-race intolerable. This sensitivity is masked from the world, perhaps with a gruff or sharp exterior, yet behind that mask is a soul who loves truth and beauty. The positive 7 can be alone but not lonely, for in his aloneness, he finds the Self, and through the Self discovers the Whole.

AFFIRMATIONS FOR 7

I go within and find my Truth.

I am never alone,
for what is true and what is good is within me.

No matter how deeply I search, I am able to
maintain my relationships with others.

8

Image	**ADMINISTRATOR/EXECUTOR**
Desire	**TO GOVERN – TO CHOOSE**
Pattern	**MASTERY – POWER**

Positive Expression
discriminating
knows choices
administration
knows value
organizing people
accomplishment
balance
judgment
decision making
ambition
intelligence
practicality
executive ability
self confidence
realism
handles finance
allocates resources
  wisely
prosperous

Negative Expression
abuse of power
controlling
over-ambitious
materialistic
callous disregard for
  others
dishonest
careless with money
domineering

Denial Expression
material unconcern
denies power
fears failure
poor judgment
no discrimination

A Positive Vision For 8

Having mastered the outer and inner worlds, the **8** now steps into the public domain to assert strong leadership and authority. This is the power of decision making, of determining the uses of energy and finance.

Developed and focused intelligence is required to fully utilize this powerful vibration. Much is demanded of this number for this is the administrator who directs and shapes organizations and governments. A person with an **8** vibration may enjoy fame, position, and wealth providing he calls upon the wisdom and knowing of the 7 and the positive aspects from all the other vibrations, especially those of responsibility, perseverance, joy of creation, savvy, cooperation and courage.

Although much is asked of her, much is also given to the worthy **8**. Opportunities abound although they may be just as easily lost. The positive **8** weighs the merits of a situation, then acts with dispatch.

AFFIRMATIONS FOR 8

*I gratefully accept my power
and use it for the good of the Whole.*

*I discriminate among options and choose
what is most constructive for myself and others.*

*I respect the energy I find in others and direct it
wisely and justly when given the opportunity.*

I have the self confidence to make important decisions.

9

Image	**THE COMPASSIONATE BUDDHA**
Desire	**TO GO BEYOND SELF -- TO RELEASE ATTACHMENT**
Pattern	**UNIVERSALITY - FORGIVENESS**

Positive Expression
altruistic
selfless giving
no attachment
universal outlook
empathy
compassion
impersonal life
completion
forgiveness
brother/sisterhood
inspired
artistically gifted
dramatic
perfection
group consciousness
synergistic

Negative Expression
no sense of self
pity
emotionality
selfish
fear of loss
fear of limitation
indiscreet
fickle
recklessly generous
intolerant
indiscriminate
explosive

Denial Expression
aimless
depressed
gullible
pessimistic
exploitable
greedy
parochial

A Positive Vision For 9

The call to go beyond the personal self and merge with a greater whole is the dynamic of **9**. Selflessness is required in order to tap into the positive beauty of this number vibration. **9s** are the spiritual dreamers, the person ready to give his last shirt to the needy as material things are less important to him than reaping blessings of the soul.

Because the mystic **9** feels and is part of each person, his sense of compassion and the drama of life is heightened. The **9** is the natural actor for all life is a drama.

Wanting to be part of the Whole, the **9** learns to release all attachments to things or people who would limit the ability to expand and merge with the Greater Self. Becoming free allows the **9** to make the world his home and to change in whatever direction is dictated by the inner self. The **9** is the humanitarian, the dreamer, the mystic, the Universal Lover.

AFFIRMATIONS FOR 9

I find myself in all people
and embrace the good which I know is there.

I face endings with equanimity as I know
every ending represents a new beginning.

I become part of something greater
than myself without losing my individuality.

Double Digit Number Families

Up to this point we have looked at the meaning of only single digit numbers. Many of the single digits, however, are the result of adding compound numbers together. By analyzing the number patterns of these compound numbers, the final number pattern contains more detail and depth.

Let us take as an example the number 8. There are many ways to add numbers together to get an 8, for instance 1+7=8, 2+6=8, or 3+5=8, etc. As an example, let us take the number 17. Look at the first number, which is 1 (or 10) and then the second number which is 7. The 7, the pattern of wisdom and research, is in the context of 10, a mental number and the pattern for invention and going into the unknown. Together they add up to the powerful pattern of 8. This 8 would therefore be colored by wisdom and self-assured authority and therefore a very different 8 from a 26/8 where both the 2 and the 6 are emotional, relationship oriented patterns. Both 8's wield authority and power, but the one might be cold and calculated whereas the other could be warm and compassionate. It is no wonder that the Philosopher King Solomon's number is 17. How could a more emotionally composed regent even suggest cutting a baby in half?

There are two families of double digit numbers which have particular significance. These families are *Master Numbers* and *Karmic Numbers*. We may reduce these double digits numbers to a single digit for the purpose of determining a final position number; however, it is important to always keep them in mind and, when reading a chart, to take the double digit into consideration.

Master Numbers

When adding numbers together the result may be the double numbers of 11, 22, 33 or 44, which are known as the Master Numbers. Some Numerologists will continue on with 55, 66, and so forth, however there are extremely few people who have those numbers in their charts, and for the purpose of this book, we have chosen to only represent the first four Master Numbers. The double numbers create a vibrational field providing the individual with increased powers to use positively or negatively.

When constructing a chart, it is normal practice to preserve the master number alongside the single digit which it creates. Example: the Master Number 22 will remain visible as 22/4. When an individual is in the Developmental Cycle (1-28 years of age), she is usually unable to make a link with the master potential in her chart. Of course there are exceptions to this rule, but for the most part, a teenage child would not have the foundation of life experience to be a master builder. By accepting and mastering the lessons of the 4, however, and becoming a person of perseverence, diligent at the nitty-gritty work before her, and exercising her fine organizational capacities, by the time she is in her Power Cycle (28 to 56 years), she could begin to demonstrate master builder qualities. But even age and experience do not guarantee this person is a *master builder* for she may still not be living up to the potential of the 22. Look at the reality of her life and see what is being accomplished and imagined before calling this individual a *master!*

11

The Master Number 11 is considered to be the person with visionary capabilities. In its lower octave as a 2 there is sensitivity, receptivity and perhaps psychic ability. When it is formed of two 1s, it indicates strength, individuality, exploration of unknown territory, within a context of sensitivity and balance. The strong individual goes into the unknown (1), perceives through his receptivity and psychic ability (2) a vision of what can be, and returns with this knowledge to inspire and stimulate others. The danger this person faces has to do with being caught in illusions or fantasies that never materialize.

22

The Master Number 22, however, is not content with mere inspiration. This is the number of the Master Builder who has the vision (the double 2) and builds (4) it into concrete form on the physical plane. Visions can be enormous or private, however the 22 is usually considered a builder on a large scale, crossing national boundaries, and building for mankind. The danger for the lazy 22 is becoming deluded with visions of grandeur not deserved or earned.

33

The Master Number 33 combines the imaginative self-expression of the 3 with the ability of the 6 to respond and nurture. This would be your Master Teacher who could guide the inquiring student into all areas of the known and unknown fields of knowledge and human experience. The fully developed 33 would be a master performer, enchanting an audience while communicating or indoctrinating the listeners into religion, politics, or whatever area the 33 chooses to guide the aspirant.

44

One could expect the fully developed 44 to be a master of industry, business, or government as the solidly established foundations of the 4, along with its capacity to endure whatever it takes with blood, sweat and tears, provide an unshakable bulwark for the 8 executive/administrative capacities. By mastering the material world, the 44 can have whatever share of power, wealth and fame he or she desires. However, the oppressive, dominating 44 could be a dictator and exploiter of human rights.

Karmic Numbers

There are diverse opinions among numerologists regarding the presence of karmic numbers. It is important to emphasize and strengthen the positive and not dwell on the negative aspect of our patterns. Nevertheless, we all know--or at least many of us believe--that we are sometimes confronted with situations for which we have no explanation. We have pain and suffering and do not know why. Karmic numbers in one's chart may offer clues as to the meaning of the pain we experience and what we can learn from it.

If the word *karmic* is new to you, its English equivalent is the "Law of Cause and Effect". Also the concept of what you sow, you reap helps us understand the meaning of karma. What we have sown may be in our current life. For Buddhists, Hindus, and metaphysicians, however, it may also come from a past life and we have chosen to correct this error in this lifetime. Think of karmic numbers as messages from our soul, helping us correct past mistakes. By understanding them in this light, they become positive indicators that we now have the strength and resources to make right what once went wrong.

The good news is that once a karmic lesson has been learned, we are no longer subject to the karma. You can now accept the lesson, learn from it and move on.

The following numbers are considered the major karmic numbers by most numerologists and, as you will see; they are all numbers within the context of the 10s, or the self, for when the self is reduced to the ego self, then it can make many mistakes.

14

There has been physical abuse (1+4=5) in the past, and the soul has chosen this lifetime to remember to take care of the body. Therefore attention is drawn to the physical body, perhaps through illness or a physical handicap of some sort. Once the karma has been accepted, you may choose to take corrective action and lead a more healthy life. Eventually your physical body will manifest radiant health, if not in this life, then in the next.

16

Having this karmic number in a prominent position upon your chart, signifies that in a past incarnation a relationship of love (6) was exploited for the benefit of the ego (1). Because of this over-bearing ego exploitation, the loved one, in this past life, was prevented from realizing his or her potential. This life, therefore, becomes the great opportunity to redeem your ability to love in a life-affirming way. The means by which this learning takes place is often through the painful experience of being left and abandoned by the one you love. If you choose to learn from this experience rather than feeling sorry for yourself or bitter, you can overcome this karmic lesson. The sum of 16 is the truth seeking 7. Meditate on the deeper meaning of your pain and you will discover that releasing the loved one to the dictates of his or her own soul, will teach you to love.

19

In the past, the ego (1) claimed everything (9) for itself without regard for the whole. This is the ultimate act of selfishness. When this karmic number turns up in a major position, it is an indication that the soul has chosen this lifetime to turn that selfishness around and to become selfless. This may be painful as the unwilling ego wants to hold onto everything for itself. But in the greater scheme of things, this is not allowed for we're all part of one being. Things and possessions must be released willingly or ripped away unwillingly. The sacrifice for the greater whole will be made. But once you discover the pleasure of giving and sharing, then the selfish desires can be transformed into selflessness.

Compound Numbers

All compound numbers can be reduced to a single digit. However, the emotional content of the single digit arising from the compound number varies according to the numbers from which it is derived. For example, take the compound number 25. The 5 is within the context of 20, so we look at the significance of 20: a 2 and a 0. The 0 tells us to add spirit to the single digit, lifting it an octave from where it was before. The 2 is a pattern of sensitivity and concern with detail; with a 0, it is the same, only more so. 5 is a physical number, always desiring to be free and to explore. The summation of 2 and 5 is the number 7, a pattern concerned with knowing, truth and inner analyses. The integration of these numbers suggests the profile of a healer: a person of sensitivity with a fine sense of detail, physical curiosity, and the scientist's analytical probing for the truth. The description of the ideal healer.

Use your own sense of logic, imagination and intuition to interpret compound numbers.

☼

Look at the centuries and decades in terms of compound numbers. You will find it a fascinating peek into history. As an example, let us consider the century we are just leaving. Although this has been called the Twentieth Century, the numbers began with 19. If you remember the meaning of the karmic 19, it may offer some insight into why this century has been so traumatic for so many. We have been in the 1900s for almost one hundred years and the loss of property and life through war and famine and the sense of sacrifice of country, physical health, fortune and so forth, has been enormous throughout the world. Yet the forces of greed and desire to exploit many for the benefit of the few has been unconscionable.

Between 1914 (the karmic 14 of physical abuse) and 1918 which includes the karmic number 16, the world suffered through the worst war in history up to that time. The hopes of a generation of women were thwarted in the scarcity of available husbands and the breakup of whole nations of people was set into process, such as the Ottoman Empire in the Near East, creating the climate for future conflict throughout the century.

We next move into the 1920s where the pattern of 2 enters into the picture. 2, as we recall, describes the pattern of peace making, negotiations, compromise and partnership. It is not by accident that attempts to create a world organization, the League of Nations, were made during this decade. The greed of the 19, however, undermined this attempt as the powerful western nations grabbed for oil and the control of territories, setting the stage for World War II and the ongoing crises in the Middle East.

The stock market crash of the late 20s brought into the 30s feeling among most that the bottom had dropped out, security was lost and the need to find parental figures, like Franklin Roosevelt and Social Welfare, to take care of the many people suddenly helpless and lacking resources. The 3, of course, is the pattern of the child who is often a victim as a result of his helpless condition and lack of maturity.

In the 1940s, the karmic relationship of loss (19) together with the physical foundation (4) of our world resulted in the most horrific war in human remembered history. This was a decade in which the first atomic bomb was dropped ('45=9 an ending to life as we had known it).

The '50s are the enigma of the century, for the 5 represents physical change yet on the surface the decade looked static. The *spirit of change*, however, was at work in the children and many of the adults–I certainly felt its power . The need to break through the barriers of tradition and find new answers for life was smoldering in many hearts and the pot boiled over in the '60s, directly challenging love, home, community, relation-ships, all aspects of the number 6. The '70s became a decade for individual and group process to understand ourselves and what had happened to us–to move away from social and into personal change.

The '80s saw the explosion of get rich and pyramidal schemes, affluence, and prosperity (8). While the decade of the

'90s, end of the century and the coming of the millennium, is filled with the sense of impending doom or deliverance. Certainly an ending, whether by fire, earthquake, flood or a failed computer system!

The new millennium, starting with the year 2000, has the 2 in the position of container for the whole period of one thousand years. The keynote of the 2 pattern is peace, understanding, support, cooperation and all the other attributes, including that of the feminine, which have been laid out in the section describing the 2 pattern. Astrology tells us that we have entered, or are entering into the Aquarian Age which is the Age of Brotherhood (and one would expect that to mean the Age of Sisterhood also!). Other voices have predicted this new age will be that of the Feminine, a time of peace and prosperity for all, not just the few as is now the case. Numerology would support these prophesies of peace and Sisterhood as the millennium is contained within the 2 Pattern. Yet to gain the whole picture we need to also look at the negative and denial aspects of the 2. In the final analysis–as this is a free-choice universe–if enough of us choose the positive side of 2, then the promises of a blessed period of peace could indeed be ours. Let us pray that we learned the lesson of the karmic 19 during this past century so that we can enjoy the potential for peace and harmony in this coming millennium.

Special Aspects of Numbers

Beyond the sequential relationship of numbers, they each have attributes which tell us more about them, giving a richness and depth of content that merely abstract numbers don't have. Such clothing of the numbers helps them come alive, creating images in our minds. In Astrology we have the mythology of the gods and goddesses to give life and drama to the astrological signs.

In Tarot there is the visual imagery of the cards, the colors, shapes, persons shown and their positions, which stimulate the right side of our brains and allow us to flesh out the meaning of the card. We need to engender similar images of the numbers in order to engage our imagination and full brain when reading a chart. So a 6 is not just a homemaker, but has an emotional, female, artistic element that she brings to the job. See this feminine or masculine element when considering a number. Sense its objective mental or warm emotional aspects.

Planes of Expressions

I discuss the chart of the Planes of Expression in more depth in Section III. However, I wish to mention them briefly now during our *clothing* of the number patterns. Each number belongs to an aspect of ourselves–our physical, emotional, mental and intuitive bodies.

Our physical body refers to that part of ourselves that engages our senses in the world of matter, whereas our emotional response to the world originates with our emotional body. The mental body is the realm of thoughts, ideas and the rational manipulation of such thoughts. The intuitional body alludes to the invisible, spiritual, and psychic realm which gathers understanding and truth beyond the mind and senses.

.   4 and 5 are physical numbers
.   3 and 6 are emotional numbers
.   1 and 8 are mental numbers
.   2 and 7 are intuitional numbers
.   9 is both emotional and intuitional, however, as it is not
        assigned to a specific letter, it would not appear in the
        Planes of Expression.

Initiations

The day of birth tells you which Life Initiation you are experiencing. If your day of birth is 25, you would be in a 7 (2+5) Initiation, which happens to be that of Water. Note in the following descriptions of the elements that they do not correspond to the elements we recognize in Astrology or other systems.

. The *Water Initiation*, which is that of education and learning, are numbers 1, 5 and 7. It is considered the easiest initiation because 1 is always the student, always in the process of learning.

. The *Air Initiation*, which is art, emotion and creativity, are numbers 3, 6 and 9. Air permeates everything, and therefore the individual with an Art Initiation could be in any area of endeavor. 3-6-9 are the Art trine.

. The *Fire Initiation*, which is through industry, business and finance, are numbers 2, 4 and 8. The Fire Initiation is the most difficult one of all, demanding one stay strongly connected with a material reality and work in the physical world.

Masculine and Feminine Numbers

. Odd numbers are masculine, restless, active and changeable.

. Even numbers are feminine, conservative and stabilize events

Denial Expression of Numbers

The number pattern on an individual's chart can be denied for there is always free choice in life. For instance, it is often puzzling to observe a person with a strong 1 position acting in a submissive and uncreative way when the 1 would suggest just the opposite behavior. This phenomena may be explained by past life karmic patterns or through the current personality's fear of expressing its inherent capacities. The denial of a position on a chart can happen if the person grows up in a repressive or dominating environment which dictates an unnatural development in the child which then evolved into the adult behavior.

The value of knowing our numbers is to make us aware of strengths we may not have realized in ourselves, or qualities we can easily draw upon for help once we are willing to release the crippling programs of I can't, I'm not good enough, or the Blame Game.

Section VI discusses the misuse of number patterns in greater depth. Your chart may clearly show where your denial expressions reside. On the other hand, as you work with your chart and find a position indicating a pattern which you reject for yourself, use this clue to challenge your belief system about yourself. If your position says you are a 1 Essence and you have limped through life identifying yourself as being weak and dependent, you have been given an invaluable tool to acknowledge your true nature: one who is inventive, courageous and individualistic. Begin to identify with the positive qualities of your number pattern; use the affirmations provided in Section II, and radiate out to the world who you truly are.

The production of this book is a result of my own discovery when I set up my chart with the Chaldean method, that my Essence is a 3 pattern--the writer, communicator. I think of all those years in which I yearned to seriously write but denied myself this outlet because I had been raised to always place the needs of others before my own, whether family or employer. I now have the ammunition I need to assert my own desire to express myself on the printed page which is not just a selfish need, but my mission in this life time. How many 1 essence women are denying their own strength and uniqueness in their belief that being submissive is the way they need to function in order to keep a relationship together?

III

MAKING IT PERSONAL:
SETTING UP YOUR CHART

Now that you have had the opportunity to study the various number patterns and have been given insight into the character of the numbers, it is time to create your own chart and discover what numbers are especially significant for you.

An Equivalency Chart is given on the following page. This chart holds the key to applying the number patterns to your name, for the sound of every letter creates a vibration which has been identified with a corresponding number. The correspondence of letter to number may differ among the various numerology systems available. I suspect we will have the precise correspondences some day, but until then I have found the current Chaldean equivalencies to provide a helpful tool for interpretation.

Retain for yourself the right to question, challenge and research this area.

EQUIVALENCY CHART

1	2	3	4	5	6	7	8
A	B	C[1]	D	E	U	O	F
I	C[2]	G	M	H	V	Z	P
J	K	L	T	N	W		
Q	R	S			X		
Y							

[1]Soft C as in certain.   [2]Hard C as in cat.

Despite your suspicions to the contrary, your name and birth date are not accidental. They provide the tools and life experiences your soul has chosen for this current life journey. It is reassuring to know that you bring with you the capacities and strengths to face whatever challenges and opportunities come to you and the talents you bring are exactly the ones you need. Not because they will enable you to skim easily over the surface of life, but because they have the possibility of taking you down into the depths where you can grasp and integrate the full meaning of your experiences, providing, as always, that you choose to exercise the opportunities placed before you. It is these experiences that can enable you to unfold your potential.

The name you were given at birth, exactly as written on your birth certificate even if it was spelled incorrectly, furnishes you with the blueprint of who you, the Journeyer, are this time around. Your name describes your essence and purpose, your driving energy, and the manner in which you present yourself to others. It delineates qualities you need to strengthen while also pointing out areas where you have an excess of energy.

In this section you will learn how to set up an analysis chart which is your basic map. As on any map, you are shown how to reach your destination, but the true flavor of that destination is not experienced until you get there. This section tells you how to get there, but the rest of the book fleshes out your destination. Keep in mind this was your chart at birth. Already the experiences of your life have had some impact, large or small, and your Table of Soul Quality Development will not reflect where you are right now, but rather the potentials inherent at your birth and what your initial life assignment was that awaited you. By the end of your first Life Cycle (28 years) you may have successfully found your balance.

There is never anything in your chart which should shame or embarrass you. We have all made mistakes and had excesses. It is the courageous soul that chooses a lifetime to correct these mistakes. Once your analysis chart has been completed look at the chart as a whole before you dissect it, position by position. Get a sense of which numbers seem to show up many times, or those which are absent. Look at which numbers show up on the main positions–are they harmonious with each other, i.e. masculine/masculine, odd/odd? Do they seem to be in conflict with each other, i.e., masculine/ feminine, odd/even? Do they reinforce each other, i.e. 1-3-5 or 2-4-8?

Resist the temptation to leap to conclusions based on one position only, like the Life Path. This is a very strong position; however, it's only part of the whole picture. No single position stands alone. Keep in mind the interactive dynamic of your chart.

Before you start mapping out your chart, make for yourself a portable number equivalency card using the Equivalency Chart on the proceeding page to obtain your numbers assigned to each letter. Have this card laminated, if at all possible, for it will be a handy tool for you to take with you to use when doing someone's numerology in the coffee shop!

Next, on a sheet of lined paper, third line down, write out your name as it appeared on your Birth Certificate. A sample chart is given on page 54. Use this for a model of the chart you will now be setting up for your own name and birthdate.

The remainder of this section will show you, step by step, how to lay out your chart and obtain the numbers which describe the ten (and more) positions. Check your addition several times as an error could create a very different interpretation of who you are and your experiences in life.

Exceptions to the Rules

. You will note there are no number 9 letters in the Chaldean system. It was the belief of these ancient scientists that the number 9, the universal number, is present within every other number. We all share this universal energy. To see how this works, add 9+4=13 and 1+3=4. When you keep adding until you have reached a single digit, you will find that you've kept your 4 but the 9 disappeared, or was rather absorbed into the 4. Try this experiment of adding the 9 to other numbers and watch it disappear. Multiplying 9 to other numbers and reducing the sum to a single digit has the same affect.

. There may be times when a so-called consonant serves in the capacity as a vowel, i.e., y. When this is the case, the y should be treated as a vowel, like in Betty. When the y is followed by a vowel, or is definitely used as a consonant, like in Yale, the rules for the consonant apply to this y.

. The case for the c is also an exception. When it is hard, like a k, it has the 2 pattern, but when it is soft like Caesar or Charles, it falls within the 3 vibrational pattern.

It may be difficult to understand why certain letters are assigned to certain numbers. In these cases we have to rely upon the traditional assignments, and even traditions vary so greatly that one can question the system entirely. As I said in the beginning, you must retain your own right to question and determine whether or not the patterns speak to you. In your own deepest heart you know the truth of yourself and this is your greatest source of authority. It is dangerous for even the most talented psychic to tell another person what he is or should be, or to swallow whole cloth the information given through the various *ologies*! Let the numbers provide you with clues rather than unalterable truth.

On the following page a complete numerology chart has been constructed for a mythical person named Linda Anne Walker. Use this chart as a model for the charts which you will be setting up for yourself and others. I have been shown other methods for constructing charts, but this particular arrangement of numbers to name and birthdate is by far the most easily read, and offers a global view of the whole person. By using a red pen to delineate major positions, the important features of the chart pop out even more prominently.

CHART FOR LINDA ANNE WALKER,
BORN JULY 10, 1943
(See Exhibit A at end of book for handwritten example chart)

```
  2       6       6     =     14 = 14/5 Heart's Desire/
  1   1   1   5   1   5                Emotional Drive
LINDA   ANNE   WALKER

3 5 4     5 5   6 3 2  2
  12       10     13
  3        1       4    =          8 Persona/Physical

31541   1555   613252
  14      16      19
  5        7       1    =     13    = 4 Essence/Intuitional
```

Table of
Soul Quality
Development

					Age	Pinnacle
1 = 4					1-29		8
2 = 2					30-39	11/	9
3 = 2			6		40-49	Power	8
4 = 1		Pinnacles	8		50-E	Goal	6
5 = 5			8 9				
6 = 1	Cycles		7 1 8	= 16/7 = Life Path		
7 = 0			July 10, 1943			
8 = 0			6 7			
	Challenges		1 Main Challenge		
			1			

Planes of Expression	Hidden Life Path (HLP)	Personal Years
Physical = 6	Life Path = 7	1997 - 16/7
Emotional = 3	Cycle = 1	1998 - 8
Mental = 4	Pinnacle = 6	1999 - 9
Intuitional = 2	HLP = **14/5**	2000 - 1

Finding Your Numbers

The Cornerstone

Your Cornerstone is the first letter or letters of your first name, which come before the first vowel. If you have more than one consonant before the first vowel, add the number equivalencies together until you obtain a single digit; i.e., in the name Charles there is the C=3 and the h=5, which together add up to 8. The first vowel of your first name, is the *delivery system* for the Cornerstone. Vowels embody the emotional soul energy we have within us, and it is this emotional energy that gives us drive. If your name begins with a vowel, such as in the name Ian, the number pattern of the vowel serves as both the Cornerstone and the energy that drives it.

In the example chart on the opposite page, the Cornerstone vibrational pattern is 3, derived from the letter L-Linda. The first vowel in Linda's name is i; thus, it is the power of 1 which provides her with her driving energy .

The Vowels
The Heart's Desire: Emotional Expression

The single digit number from the total of the vowels in your name is your **Heart's Desire** number. To find this number, add together the vowel numbers occurring in the individual names until you have arrived at a single digit for each name. Once the single digit for each separate name has been accomplished, add these together to obtain a number for all the names. If a compound number is the result, this is reduced to a single digit, but keep the compound number in tact for future reference, especially if it is a master or karmic number.

$$
\begin{array}{ccc}
2 & 6 & 6 \\
1 \quad 1\ 1 & 5 & 1 \quad 5
\end{array}
\qquad = 14 = 1+4 = 14/5
$$

Example: LINDA ANNE WALKER

The Consonants
The Persona: Physical Expression

As with the vowels, add the consonant numbers for each name until you arrive at a single digit for each name and then add those numbers up to obtain the single digit Persona number.

Example: LINDA ANNE WALKER
$$
\begin{array}{ccc}
3\ 5\ 4 & 5\ 5 & 6\ \ 3\ 2\ 2 \\
12 & 10 & 13 \\
3 & 1 & 4 \quad = 8
\end{array}
$$

Combined Consonants and Vowels
The Essence: Intuitive Self

It's tempting to add together the single digits of Soul and Persona numbers to derive the Essence number, however you may be missing important master number or karmic number clues if you do so. Therefore, on a separate line, bring down all the number equivalencies of both vowels and consonants below your line of consonant numbers and add these up for each individual name until you have a single digit for each name. Notice how the karmic 14, 16, and 19 appear in her Essence position.

Example: LINDA ANNE WALKER
$$
\begin{array}{ccc}
315\ 4\ 1 & 1\ 5\ 5\ 5 & 6\ 1\ 3\ 2\ 52 \\
14 & 16 & 19 \\
5 & 7 & 1
\end{array}
\qquad 13 = 1+3 = 4
$$

Soul Quality Development

Refer to Linda's chart. You will notice that down the left side there is a listing of numbers 1 through 8 followed by an equal sign. This is the **Soul Quality Development** position. Create a list like this on your paper, adding up all the individual numbers on your Essence line, (i.e., the number of 1s, 2s, etc.) and place the quantity for each number behind the equal sign for that number. For instance, Linda has four 1s in her chart, two 2s, and so forth down to zero 8s.

Missing Numbers
If a number is missing among the letters in your name, indicate that by writing a 0 after the number. Include only the actual letter/number equivalencies and not any of the compound or final position results (i.e., Heart's Desire, etc.).

Excessive Numbers
On the other hand, if you have more than three of a particular number, determine which numbers those are by highlighting them in some form or another. (note: The number 5 is an exception to this rule as it is considered the number of humanity. More than five 5's, however, represents an excess.)

Planes of Expression

Another way of defining the number qualities is how they relate to our four bodies: the physical, emotional, mental and intuitional. The quantity of a number pattern indicates not only how much energy is going into this pattern, but how that particular body will express itself. As an example, a 1 is considered a mental number pattern and rules the mind. Therefore, if someone has ten 1's in their name, they would express their mental body with inventiveness, would initiate and design new projects, and not be afraid to be individualistic in their thinking. Furthermore, with ten 1's, their mental energy would be enormously powerful–probably too much for those around them. However, if the name discloses only one 1, the mental pattern would be the same but without the force and self-confidence of the individual having the ten 1's in their name.

Count the letters in the name for each one of the Planes of Expression and enter that quantity next to the body it represents.

Physical Expression	4's and 5's
Emotional Expression	3's and 6's
Mental Expression	1's and 8's
Intuitional Expression	2's and 7's

Some numerologists consider the 2 an emotional expression, which it is, however the sensitivity and receptivity of the 2 creates an intuitional climate, especially if it comes through the 11. You may wish to consider the 2 as both emotional and intuitional

Birthdate - Life Path

In the middle of the lined paper, write in your birth date, using all the numbers for the birth year. I will illustrate all number positions from the birthdate by referring to Linda's chart, page 54. Above the month, write in the single digit for the month (i.e., November would be 11=1+1=**2**), then the single digit for the day number, and the single digit year number. Add these together to get a single or compound number. If the number is compound, add those numbers to derive a single digit. This single digit number is called the **Life Path** number.

Remember to retain master or karmic significance, as in the example from Linda's chart.

	7 - 1 - 8	=	16 = **7 or 16/7**
Example:	7 - 10 - 1943		
	July 10, 1943		

Cycles

The numbers of your month, day and year of birth are considered your **Life Cycles** on the chart. Your month of birth is your Developmental Cycle, the day of birth is your Power Cycle, and the year of birth is your Wisdom Cycle. (Refer to page 96 for more information on determining age.)

    Example: July 10, 1943
             7   1   8   =   **cycles.**

Pinnacles

As in the example shown below, add together your month and day of birth which gives you your first Pinnacle. Now add your day of birth and year of birth. This is your second Pinnacle. Add your first and second Pinnacles together to discover your third Pinnacle. Finally, add your month of birth and year of birth to arrive at your fourth Pinnacle. (Refer to page 100 for more information on computing age.)

Example:		6		=	
		8		=	**Pinnacles**
	8		9	=	
	7	1	8		
	July	10	1943		

Challenges

Subtract your month from your day of birth. This gives you your first Challenge. Subtract your day of birth from your year of birth to find your second Challenge. Subtract your first and second Challenges from each other to derive your third, and **Main Challenge**. Subtract your month number from your year number to obtain your fourth and final Challenge.

```
Example      July  10  1943
              7    1    8
                 6    7      ⎫
                   1         ⎬ Challenges
                   1         ⎭
```

Power Goal Number

Add together the Essence and Life Path numbers and reduce to a single digit. This is your **Power Goal Number.**

Example: Essence Number   = 4
          Life Path Number   = 7
          Power Goal Number   = **11/2**

Hidden Life Path Number

Add the Life Path number together with the current Cycle and current Pinnacle. The sum, reduced to a single digit, is the Hidden Life Path number. As in Linda's chart, 7 Life Path + 1 Cycle (1971-1999) + 6 Pinnacle (1993 to Present) = **14/5,** the Hidden Life Path Number.

Universal Year

Add the current year numbers to derive a single digit, i.e., $1998 = 1+9+9+8 = 27 = 2+7 = 9$. 9 is the Universal Year.

Personal Year

Add your first **Pinnacle** to the **Universal Year** to derive your Personal Year. On Linda's chart, her first pinnacle is **8**, and 8 plus the Universal Year of 1998 (9) is $8+9=17$, and $1+7= **8**$. **8** is Linda's Personal Year for 1998.

Personal Month

Add your Personal Year with the number of the month (i.e., January $=1$, February $=2$, and so forth) to discover what number pattern rules your month.

Personal Day

Add the number of the day to your personal month to discover your personal day. For instance, if you are in a 5 month and it is the 3rd day of the month, your personal day would be an 8 which is the summation of $5+3$.

Conclusion

All the numerical information for interpreting your Numerology Chart has now been set out before you. You can see how easy it has been to discover your own numbers. There has been no need to use a calculator, look up information in an Ephemerid, or have a degree in mathematics!

The focus for the rest of this book will be on learning what all these positions have to say to you—who you are and why your life is played out differently from another person's life. The visual image of the completed chart keeps you aware of the bigger picture and helps you to not become too identified with any one position. As you have learned, some number patterns seem to harmonize with each other while others have a stressed or conflicting relationship. Observing where those patterns are on your chart will allow you to start taking charge of your inner and outer conflicts.

Okay, go for it. If you feel bogged down at any point, remember, what we seem to be right now is only a very, very small part of our total magnificent Self. But this is the part we have come to work on, so work on it with acceptance, love, and imagination. Every number pattern has the capacity to take you to the stars or into the pits. You always have the choice!

IV

THE POSITIONS IN YOUR NAME

Introduction

Buckle your seat belt! You are about to start the biggest adventure of your new life. If your soul has been hanging around in heaven waiting for an opportunity to jump into a new body, then before the big leap takes place some important decisions have to be made, such as : what will I look like and what will be my purpose? What should I put in my *tool kit* for survival? Your name will reveal answers to these questions and more. It's all in the numbers.

We looked at the stories numbers tell in Section II and developed a good sense of how each number calls to it the subsequent vibrational pattern. In Section III we learned how to find the numbers for the ten positions on the numerology chart. All of this is necessary ground-work for reaching the point where you can finally flesh that theoretical information out with your own personal scenario.

As you begin this process, keep in mind that you are a whole, living system. Dissecting a life can be misleading if you get stuck on a part that may seem more glamorous, or tragic, while ignoring the boring or unattractive parts. All the details of your life are like pieces of a jigsaw puzzle needing to be fitted together so the true picture can emerge. What may seem strong in a specific position, may be neutralized or modified in the chart as a whole. And what may seem boring may be your saving grace!

The Cornerstone

The definition for "cornerstone" found in the American College Dictionary states,

> 1. a stone which lies at the corner of two walls, and serves to unite them,
> 2. a stone built into a corner of the foundation of an important edifice as the actual or nominal starting point in building, usually laid with formal ceremonies, and often hollowed out and made the repository of documents, etc.,
> 3. something of fundamental importance.

Numerology draws upon all three of these meanings since the pattern of the Cornerstone position is of fundamental importance in a person's life. It is an interesting thought that lying within this Cornerstone, may be the contract for this lifetime determined prior to the individual's birth. The Cornerstone would provide the key to the nature of the contract, and perhaps the spirit within which one's life needs to be lived.

Let us look at the first definition of the Cornerstone serving as the unification point for two walls, thereby setting the orientation of the building. The two walls on the chart are the Essence and the Life Path. For instance, the Cornerstone of Linda is the 3 pattern. 3 suggests Linda made a fundamental decision before incarnating to use imagination, joy and artistic expression as an orientation for her life. Her 7 Life Path demands she go within herself to find her truth, while her 4 Essence shows her to be a practical, hardworking person. Introducing lightness and fun into her life would enable her to be more balanced and whole.

At this point we haven't discussed the meaning of the Life Path and the Essence positions, however, you have looked at the number meditations and can see that both the 4 and the 7 patterns denote a no-nonsense attitude, yet seem to be incompatible with each other. The 4 is concerned with solid matter, while the 7 deals in the subtler realms of the mind and spirit. It is the tensions between these two seemingly contradictory patterns which require Linda to tap into her inner resourcefulness for integration, while the joy and playfulness of the 3 Cornerstone enables her to express her life with more grace.

Below are brief descriptions of how your Cornerstone could function in your life. Refer to Section II for a more complete understanding of the numbers.

Meanings For Cornerstone Patterns

1   Individuality, invention, courage, self determination.

2   Cooperation, detail concern, receptivity, peace-making.

3   Joyful imagination, creative expression, manifestation.

4   Industry, structure, loyalty, organization, hard worker.

5   Change, freedom, sociability, physical curiosity, versatility.

6   Family, service, relationships, community, responsibility.

7   Scientific investigation, analysis, wisdom, faith.

65

8   Power, discrimination, choice, administration, authority.

First Vowel Meanings

A: No. 1   Expresses your Cornerstone energy with a courageous and resourceful pioneering spirit, coming up with inventive solutions and movement into a new physical space.

E: No. 5   Expresses your Cornerstone energy in a spirit of adventure and curiosity, as you enthusiastically explore your world and all that is in it.

I: No. 1   Expresses your Cornerstone energy with assertiveness and focused intent, moving into new mental spaces. There is a laser like quality in this 1 pattern.

O: No. 7   Expresses your Cornerstone energy with the intent to research fully, know truthfully, and utilize the wisdom of the inner Self. It is self-contained.

U: No. 6   Expresses your Cornerstone energy in the spirit of idealism, humanitarian service and mature responsibility.

An Example

Kristine's Cornerstone is the combined K (2) and R (2), which add up to the 22 Master Builder pattern, delivered and expressed by the vowel "I" which is a 1. The unique marriage she is in has taught her how to be independent rather than looking to her husband for support. Her Life Path number is also the 22, corresponding with her Cornerstone number; it is also an indication she is challenged by the need to master the material world in order to manifest something as far reaching as the potential of the 22. This may prove difficult for her as her Essence and Persona are both the 3 pattern, which can be the impetuous child, charming but undisciplined. However, the necessities of being a mother and wife and her passion for crafts and writing songs which fulfill the spirit of the child, has helped her to learn to internalize the structure and perseverance required of the 4, which is the basic quality of her Life Path. She has had to cope with enormous tension, always present in her life, forcing her to reach within herself for spiritual strength and inspiration, which are the gifts of number 7. Her 3 Essence and 22/4 Life Path add up to the single digit 7, which is her Power Goal or Maturity number. Through the creative tension she experiences, she gains the wisdom that will shine ever more presently in her life as she grows older. Although still in her mid-30s, her spiritual presence and wisdom strongly affect all who meet her.

Essence - Intuitive Self - Life Purpose

Have you ever wondered why you are here on Planet Earth; what your purpose might be? If so, you probably have lots of company. It's a question many of us ask ourselves many times over in the course of our lives. There are two positions on the Numerology chart addressing this question. One of them is the Life Path, which we will discuss in Section V. The other position is the Essence position. Our Essence tells us how we respond intuitively to experiences, informing us about our purpose and mission for being here. It seems that when we are able to truly be ourselves, we fulfill our life purpose.

Knowing that we do indeed have a contribution to make by being ourselves is good news but brings us to the next question: *Who am I?*

Why should we have to ask that question at all?

Unfortunately we live in a world, a society and a culture, that lays so many trips on us about what we should be and do, and what we shouldn't be and do, that we may end up totally confused about who we really are. And if we have a sneaking suspicion about who we really are but it doesn't fit the accepted plan laid out for us by our parents, friends or society, then we may not have the courage to be ourselves.

Not being ourselves is a serious problem, however, because who we really are keeps slipping through the cracks insisting on being recognized. When it is not expressed consciously, then it will probably burst out negatively [see Section VI]. So we might as well accept our natural essence and discover its constructive expression. It will be amazing how much more pleasant life can be as a result. If you find yourself playing out the denial aspect of this pattern, then one of the most important things you can do in life is to change the polarities from negative/denial to its positive expression. Use the Affirmations in Section II, Uncovering the Number Patterns, for transforming your negatively expressed Essence number into one of positive success.

In Section IV you learned how to obtain your Essence number, which is the summation of vowels and consonants in your name. Take a look at it now. Does the way you automatically respond to a situation, and what you feel you can do, best correspond with your Essence number? Does the Essence number put you in touch with a part of you which has been repressed or denied up to now?

Brief descriptions of the Essence pattern are given below. Refer to Section II, Uncovering the Number Patterns, for a more thorough discussion of this pattern.

Essence Descriptions

1

Intuitively you are a natural explorer and pioneer into new areas of human endeavor. You tackle challenges with courage, focus, determination and with an independent and creative mind. Assertive and resourceful, you provide strength and leadership for others. Don't let that powerful determination run roughshod over others!

2

You have an intuitive ability to balance and see both sides of an issue which makes you a natural peacemaker and diplomat. You are receptive to the ideas of others, sift through them with your great sense of detail, and find the compromises and synthesis that allows opposite factions to come to agreement through your power of communication. Stick to your own truth, for you could be easily swayed by a powerful 1!

> *On the higher octave of 2, the 11, you are a visionary, one whose strongly developed sensitivity glimpses a finer possibility of life and a view of spiritual essence and beauty which you wish to communicate to others. You could be lost in illusions and addictions unless you stay grounded. As we have learned, the higher you climb, the farther you can fall!*

3

You have an intuitive capacity for joy and expression and are capable of tapping into your imagination and bringing a sense of play into even the most dull situation. Artistic expression, especially through words, is a natural release for your spontaneous disposition. You are here to uplift seriousness and gloom with your unquenchable spirit. You have the ability to manifest with greater ease than most, as your ability to imagine and believe are stronger than those of the other number patterns. Don't let your imagination run away with you, however, creating monsters that really don't exist!

4

At essence, you are conservative, the backbone and mainstay of your family and workplace. When others run away to play, you stick to the job at hand, bringing organization, method and structure. Your loyalty, integrity, and sense of justice are appreciated, however your willingness to work hard may be abused by others less industrious. And even though you enjoy working, lift your head up from time to time to enjoy the stars and catch a bigger view.

> *On a higher octave, the 22, you are the Master Builder, psychically tuned into the realm of spirit with the ability to translate that information into physical structure and form. If this is your Essence, you must beware of deluding yourself with your perceived sense of grandeur, but stay grounded in the truth of what is.*

5

You intuitively seek to expand yourself and to enlarge the sense of wonder and curiosity in those who have less scope and adventure to their lives than you have. You love travel and exposure to all that's new and unusual, with an eagerness to learn and know all about this fabulous world we live in. And you love to share your excitement about life with others, for you are a natural talker and the life of the party. Watch your restlessness, your fondness for sexual entanglements and your unwillingness to make a commitment! You are here to experience the arena of physical life, but not everyone is as fluid as you are.

6

Your nurturing capacity is natural and boundless. You take in the homeless animals and little children with dirty hands and faces, if not literally, then figuratively. You have a natural desire to teach, to pass on information, whether it be recipes or art techniques. Culture is based upon the sense of community and institution which you hold within yourself. A patron of the arts, you create healing and nurturing environments, and handle responsibility with grace. Because you have such high ideals, you can feel betrayed when others do not live up to what you believe they should be. Your fine sense of how things should be may slip into bigotry or judgmentalness. Always allow others to follow their own inner truth. Remember, every person must be accepted for themselves with no expectations and comparisons. Beware of jealousy or possessiveness.

7

You never accept anything at face value but want to probe and analyze and verify for irrefutable proof. The desire to know drives you into science, religion, and/or metaphysics. You find answers within yourself as you surround yourself with solitude, nature and beauty. Others may find you hard to understand, indeed, you may find yourself hard to understand. For you are the one who mines the gold of the inner wisdom, discovering the Truth lying below the surface where only those equipped with a prepared mind and strong desire will go. Although you find a state of detachment desirable for your inner searches, always remember you are part of the human race and you do not need to be alienated or alone! Use your drive for perfection judiciously, not violating the sensitivities and choices of others.

8

You have an intuitive power and authority which others look to when needing leadership and judgment. You can be counted upon to keep your head when others may be losing theirs, for your perspective is broader, your experience is greater, and, if you are a prepared 8, your knowledge is vaster. Wielding the power of the 8 is not for fearful people, for much will be asked of you, yet you would probably not want less from life. You enjoy playing with power and money--or its symbolic equivalent--and do this naturally. You probably have a philosophical disposition and can discriminate with your keen mind. Stay grounded and fearless, affirming your sense of appropriateness, and make your Higher Self your partner to keep your perspective clear and honest. Be careful to not misuse your power by exploiting or manipulating others less assured than yourself.

9

The World is yours and you are the World. With an empathetic emotional body tuned into the drama of others, as well as your own never ending drama, you discover yourself in whomever you are with and they find in you a sympathetic friend. You love the world and all the world loves you. Wherever you find yourself, you are at home. One of the artistic trine of 3-6-9, your artistic expression finds itself most fully in drama for you can sense and express the emotions of others. In its most positive expression, the 9 is selfless and compassionate, you blend with the Whole. Yet, as Humans, we are here to raise our sense of identity and selfhood to its highest expression, not to lose ourselves in the soap operas of our lives or those of other people. Hang onto your sense of individuality while merging into the whole of Humanity and the Universe.

Heart's Desire - Emotional Self

Have you ever found yourself in the position of having an important job to do but your heart wasn't in it? Perhaps you found yourself fatigued by the effort of forcing yourself into something you really didn't want to do.

Or, conversely, you whizzed through a job, accomplishing more than you believed possible because you felt such keen joy in what you were doing.

Wouldn't it be great if we could direct our passionate energy into whatever we did and experience the pleasure and ease that comes with doing what we want to do? We would be masters of our lives if this were the case, amazing others with our expertise and skill. If we understood our Heart's Desire, which is our emotional expression, and learned to harness that great power and energy, then whatever we did would be done with more enthusiasm, zest and pleasure.

Why don't we do this naturally? If we were natural people, we would. Many of us, however, may not even be aware of what our Heart's Desire is—the fuel that keeps us going. We may not have had the luxury of allowing ourselves to validate our emotional desires because of the need to please a parent or a teacher. Our drive to explore the unknown may have been nipped in the bud by a fearful parent before we had developed a strong enough ego to hold us true to our own knowing. In many cases our emotional need to have peace at any cost may supercede our need to be true to ourselves. This betrayal of ourselves may be for the simple reason of staying on the good side of the person who holds our survival in their hands! We may have been too young to know how to protect our deepest needs while remaining on the good side of that important other person.

So we find ourselves stuck and unable to honor our emotional nature, our Heart's Desire. Life takes on a uniform greyness and we wonder when our passion died. By finding the courage to acknowledge and express our true Heart's Desire, knowing that no one has the right to tell us how we should feel, we can resurrect our passion and once again discover the joy of life. The soul uses the passion and fuel in the Heart's Desire to help us evolve.

Below are brief descriptions of how the number patterns might function through the Heart's Desire. For a more expanded understanding of this pattern, refer to the number meditations in Section II. If you find yourself acting out of the denial or negative side of your pattern, work with the Affirmations for that number, or create your own affirmation. By harnessing your vital emotional energy, your life can become so much more exciting and savory.

Heart's Desire Patterns

1

You want to use your powerful mind to invent, to create something different and new. Your eagerness to go into the unknown drives you and others. You want to assert your individuality, to stand independently and not have others tell you what to do. You want to figure it out for yourself. Subservience could drive you crazy and you must be able to communicate your need for independence to others. That does not mean being alone, but it does mean being able to honor your individualistic contribution.

2

You want to work and live in partnership with others. Your desire for harmony in the home and workplace is paramount, for you dislike tension and discord. You have a passion for details and may want to have collections of anything from stamps to antiques. Your ability to tune into others makes you keenly aware of them and therefore you are a communicator who can anticipate the needs of others. You radiate a sense of nurturing and peace, wishing to stay in the background, smoothing out the rough places.

3

Like a child, you want joy and companionship, fun and laughter, song and dance. You want to be imaginative, to be outrageous, to indulge your fantasy and imagination, to be the Trickster, the performer, anything but serious and responsible. Freedom to express yourself is essential to your well-being, and putting a damper on that is a sure way to kill your passion. Fortunately it will resurrect if you acknowledge the child in you, give it room to play and express every day, reward it after it's been grounded, and know that this delightful aspect of life is just as important as the serious 9 to 5 worker. If you can find employment that draws upon this imaginative inner Child, you have it made!

4

You find your passion in structure, organization and accomplishment of tasks, of being the dependable member of your community and for being acknowledged for the work you do. You like to achieve the hard tasks, get in and dig the ditches, lay bricks, construct houses, grow food. Your passion is that of a builder, working with solid materials and building strong foundations. You are the one who works weekends for fun, not because you have to. When you see the miracle of something being built by your hands, your life energy begins to pour forth with enthusiasm. You have a passion for hard facts, rationality and understanding truth, and you feel lost and flounder in fantasy and the abstract.

5

The pull of the road is your passion! You love adventure, excitement, the adrenaline rush. Your curiosity about life calls you out of a stable existence into discovery, movement, knowledge, particularly sensual knowledge, for the 5 pattern controls the five senses. You must have freedom to satisfy this passion for exploration, and if you are bound by four walls, you could feel suffocated and smothered. Find a way to fulfill your 5 urge for discovery in your weekends and evenings, and you may uncover your squelched passion, bringing more energy back into your life.

6

What motivates you may be found in dishing out soup to the hungry, teaching young minds ethics and morality, planning a walk-a-thon to promote art, serving on a school board. Your passion comes from uplifting culture and caring for those in need. You reach out for the responsible jobs, not for the feeling of importance, but because you have the desire to make things work right and you believe you have it in you to do just that. Your passion is stimulated when you can reach out into your community or home, and provide the humanitarian service that you wish to give so generously.

7

You wish to probe deeply into the mysteries of life, to know the underlying causes of things, to dissect and analyze whether it's frogs or philosophy. This is the passion that drives you. You yearn for the quiet, uninterrupted spaces that allow your contemplative spirit to explore the unknown regions of the inner world, and you withdraw from the crowds and the noisy cacophony that disturbs your mental tranquility. If you have a 7 Heart's Desire Pattern and your passion is missing, find a mountain top or an ocean beach and spend time with yourself. Learn to meditate and draw upon your inner power.

8

The energy that fuels your life comes from being out in the world in the busy, vital marketplace where you, the entrepreneur par excellence, are wheeling and dealing with high finance and great projects. Perhaps your life has not equipped you with the opportunity to wheel and deal, but you need to find some venue for exercising your executive desires and for tapping into your emotional, Heart's Desire energy. Perhaps an organization needs a president or a financial officer. It may only be in the local P.T.A. But by getting involved in an executive capacity of some nature, you can revive your passion for life.

9

Mingling with all kinds of people and being in all kinds of places will harness your passion. Indeed, your passion for life can be so overwhelming, that you need to master it and direct it in humanitarian ways, for this is what your Heart desires. Whenever you are able to create a greater sense of connectedness among people and groups, help them to discover their relationship to the Whole, then you feel a deep sense of satisfaction. Your vitality is energized as you mix and merge with others and discover yourself in all of life. You live for those potent, emotional, dramatic moments.

Persona - the Physical Expression

Have you spent time trying to figure out what to wear to an important event? Since it is known that first impressions are crucial and made within the first seven seconds, you have decisions to make. How do you want people to experience you? How do you want to feel about yourself? Do you want to come across as a jock, an intellectual, an Earth mother, a corporate executive? And how will your appearance advance you in the way you want to go?

Can't you imagine the soul hemming and hawing in front of the Cosmic Clothes Closet to decide what to wear before taking the plunge into a physical body? This may seem like a ridiculous notion, yet how often we are told by spiritual teachers that our physical bodies are just a suit of clothes worn by the soul. A name has been given to this clothing; it is called the Persona. It is the personality in physical form which a person presents to the world. This is how that person wants others to see and experience him or her. Because it is the part of ourselves which is out in front, we can sometimes believe this is who we really are. And to some extent we are the characteristics of our Persona. Otherwise we would not be able to project it at all into the world. However, this is only our covering, and knowing and understanding this differentiation is essential. For if we identify fully with our covering, we may overlook the Essence of who we truly are and deny our Heart's Desire.

As you look over the number meditations in Section II, imagine what a person would look like for each one of the numbers. How would they dress, fix their hair, their state of cleanliness or rumpled appearance? How would they talk and communicate? What words would they choose to use? Would they be an introvert or extrovert, right in your face, or hanging around in the background? What type of car would they prefer to drive? How would they decorate their room, office, or home?

Allow yourself to imagine the appearance and personality of a number 3, a number 7, a 6. Your own creative thinking and imagining is far more powerful than my spelling out for you this information.

By now you will be gaining a sense of the different number patterns and the Persona position is perhaps the best one of all for you to play with in figuring out how they work. Sometimes these personas can be subtle in putting across their pattern, primarily because of a need to be appropriate to the setting. But somewhere there will be a clue, a give away, whether it be a loud tie in an otherwise correct black suit ensemble, a book of Shakespeare conspicuously in view, bumper stickers, whatever. We want people to experience us in certain ways and we will nearly always drop hints and clues in our clothing, our words, or our body language.

Below are some of the ways that the number pattern might express itself in the Persona position:

Persona Descriptions

1

Daredevil, risk taker, inventive, resourceful, do it all by myself, individualistic dresser.

2

Considerate, easy going, soft, sees all points of view and can't make any of her own. Dresses in such a way that no one will be challenged.

3

Vivacious, imaginative, feelings easily hurt, scatters him/herself and dresses in a playful way, though perhaps pretty unconsciously.

4

Organized, hardworking, unimaginative in clothing, but practical and suitable for occasion. Callouses on hands and muscular from hard work.

5

Flighty, exciting and excitable, on the go, sensuous and colorful clothing, out for thrills, promoter and a talker.

6

Mother Earth, responsible, wants everyone to be comfortable and safe, protective, conservative dresser.

7

Mysterious, creates opportunities to be alone in his perfect world, puts out a mask to cover real feelings, would dress with perfection, however that is defined.

8

Takes over leadership opportunities, powerful and authoritative, dresses in a corporate style, or equivalent for whatever group she wants to lead. Appears successful, takes charge.

9

Dresses in ethnic clothing or something that would make a statement about being a global citizen. A hugger, compassionate and inclusive person.

Summing It Up

Numerology has looked at and described three main attributes within the name of the Journeyer: the Essence, the Heart's Desire and the Persona. These attributes contain vital information about the nature of the Journeyer–not what he or she is *doing*, rather the *presence* or *beingness* of this person. These positions, together with the Table of Soul Quality Development (page 110) give awareness of innate talents, possibilities and predilections, and also show the areas of conflict, potential denial and the qualities needing to be recognized, bolstered and strengthened.

But a person does not live in a vacuum. If that were the case we could all imagine ourselves as being perfect in every way! Rather, it is in the confrontation with Life's challenges and demands on our every day journey that we are informed about our current reality and where we need to develop. It is the experiences that occur in our lives that stretch us to our greatest possible potential. Life is a mirror as well as an exacting teacher.

The Journeyer has checked her gear, made sure all supplies are on hand, and is now ready to discover the adventures in store for her along her soul-chosen path. Section V continues the saga, providing the details of the journey. Proceed with awareness!

V

THE POSITIONS
IN YOUR BIRTH DATE

Introduction

Things happen to us. Opportunities, challenges, and experiences often seem to drop into our laps whether we want them or not and then we are faced with the task of dealing with these events. If we allow them to, these experiences can awaken us into fuller consciousness until we reach the powerful position of choice. Choice allows us to become co-creators in our lives. We choose how we will respond to events: with vigor, bringing order out of a chaotic situation, or by deciding to set them on the back burner until we have gained more experience and knowledge for dealing with them.

Conversely, we can decide not to choose and then find ourselves driven by events which intrude, often painfully, into our lives. Eventually we learn one way or the other. Creation is patient!

These things that happen to us are described in the positions of the Life Path (Creative Mind), which includes the Life Cycles, Pinnacles, and Personal Challenges. In many systems of numerology, it is the Life Path which is given primary importance, with some systems including only this position. However, I have chosen to bring it into the overall picture secondarily to the positions described in the name.

Your name describes the contents of your *tool box*: the talents you have, the strengths you show, and your orientation towards life. It is these tools, given at birth, which enable you to successfully handle whatever comes to you providing you use them.

The events that happen to you over your lifetime, as suggested by your Life Path pattern, afford rich opportunities for developing greater awareness. As ignorance is dispelled, you find you can master problem areas which seemed so perplexing and mystifying before.

It is vital to know who we are in order for us to confront the challenges in our life with intelligent understanding.

Life Path

Imagine yourself at an intersection with nine roads leading off in different directions, each one offering a unique perspective and specific challenges which, when faced and dealt with, will carry you to your goal at the end of the road. As you attempt to select which road to take, you study your personal list of assets and liabilities: "Let's see, I'm strong in following adventure, but I'm really weak in handling responsibility." Then you study the nine roads and discover that on road number 6 you will learn about responsibility. "Ah ha," you say, "if I go down road 6 I'll be given experiences teaching me what I want to learn."

So you set off down road 6, take on a physical body and promptly forget you made a choice. Furthermore, when 6 experiences begin to appear down the road, you complain, "I don't want responsibility. I just want to be free and not have to answer to anyone." However, remember, you're on road number 6 now and you can't go back, only forward, and that means dealing with 6 experiences.

Positively accepting your Life Path number allows you to magnetize positive and wonderful experiences into your life. Resistance or denial cause the experiences to become more powerfully persuasive. Eventually you are backed into a corner and the only way out is to accept and learn the lesson of the pattern. If you remember that you chose this Path and why, your experiences will be so much sweeter.

Basically, your Life Path tells you how you can evolve spiritually. Applying those qualities to the events in your life moves you gracefully through the events, repaying karmic debts and balancing out your deficiencies.

The impact of the Life Path number is strong and compelling. On finding what your Life Path number is, look at your Soul Qualities Development chart. Is your Life Path number missing? Is it weak? Is it overly strong? Also look at your Heart's Desire and Essence patterns. Does your Life Path number show up there? Does it conflict with those patterns? Harmonize with them?

By checking out your Life Path number with all other major influences in your chart, you will immediately discover how smooth your ride is going to be in life or if you'll be challenged by rough waters! If you discover yourself in the rapids, look to your tool chest of talents and skills and find a way to make your conflicts work for your highest good. The energy created by tension is a powerful fuel for facilitating rapid growth.

Life Path Patterns

1

A spirit of adventure and boldness is required of you. You must find the courage within yourself to stand on your own, assert your independence and creative powers. Although you may have others in your life, you are the one designated to provide strength, assurance and leadership. You desire freedom to move out on your own and chart unknown territories of the mind as well as in the physical world.

On the other hand, you may want to deny this challenge of 1 and lean on others, allowing them to make decisions you need to be making for yourself. If this is the case, you may find yourself unable to hold down a job, a marriage, or whatever it is that requires you to stand firm and strong. By recognizing your need to take those experiences handed to you by life as your opportunity to develop your own strength, individuality, and courage, you will have taken an important step towards mastering your Life Path.

The positive manifestation of a 1 is self-assurance, self-directedness, self acceptance and knowledge. The negative manifestation is the demanding, overbearing, domineering and dictatorial behavior which arises from attempting to force your own way at the expense and exploitation of others.

As you desire the freedom to make your own decisions and not have to constantly be compromising your ideas with others, you are a prime candidate for being your own boss and having your own business. This does not mean you are unable to work with others, it only means you need to be in a position where you can assert your own ideas and choices.

2

With this Life Path you are being asked to be one of the peacemakers in the world, to develop the empathy that allows you to understand varying points of view and in doing so, create an environment of cooperation. To successfully perform this role, you will need to be receptive, non-judgmental, attentive to details and gain a fine sense of fairness and proportion. You are not the one to lead the way, but to support, encourage, nurture, and be a strategist to provide information to the one who does have that role. You are being given the gift of intuition and sensitivity with the 2 Life Path, and your willingness to accept this gift allows you to be one of the healers of strife and violence in the world.

By denying this function of the 2, you may find yourself being a doormat for others, or conflicting with them by your insistence on doing things your way. You become the victim, dependent on others, filled with self-pity and a sense of being weak and helpless. Because 2 is concerned with detail, a negative 2 can get lost, not seeing the forest for the trees. By recognizing that receptivity sometimes feels like weakness, and cooperation may feel like giving in, you gradually discover the path of 2 and the ability to work in partnership with others.

You are happiest when working with others in partnership, bringing your own fine sense of attunement and detail to the group. You are an asset to any group providing you are operating from the positive 2.

3

The spirit of joy and creative self-expression is yours to master and to offer others. In a world which often takes itself too seriously and is puffed up with importance and dignity, you can play the role of the clown and the joker, or just the good humored child that pops the balloons of inflated ego and allows everyone to discover the joy of being themselves. You want fun and companionship and you are given the ability to bring imagination and spontaneity to whatever situation in which you find yourself. You love to express yourself through words, in speaking or writing, for the gift of this Life Path number is that of manifestation—to bring into the physical world the germinated ideas of the Number 1.

Squelching this imaginative inner child in order to remain the serious adult may cause this magical aspect of yourself to emerge in childish ways: by being overly sensitive to perceived critical judgment, by being foolish, scattered, irresponsible, insensitive or tiresome. Being willing to use your creative imagination and self expression when it is appropriate, allows you to achieve the positive 3, becoming the joy bringer.

The pattern of the 3 is an indiscriminate one, spilling out energy just as a flower sends out its perfume regardless of who is or who is not around. There is no discernment in the nature of the child, an appealing state of innocence and beauty, but one that can be its undoing by those who exploit gullible souls. Fortunately you will find strength, maturity and cautiousness present in your tool box to protect you from being manipulated, providing you are guarded through your self-knowledge. No experience is ever given to us for which we are not well prepared. Always remember you have what it takes to turn everything into a positive situation.

Working with others in creative and artistic endeavors would be the arena which would allow you to most successfully channel your imagination and flood of ideas. Teachers are able to hold the imagination of their students when gifted with this Life Path and have the words and humor to sustain attention and enjoyment of their class.

4

Industrious work, organization, grounding and foundation building is your successful path through life when holding the 4 Life Path. Depending upon your other number patterns, you may find this desirable or stifling, nevertheless, focusing your energy into physical work provides you with the strong base for personal and spiritual growth. You are not a spiritual being in a physical world by accident, but are here to understand the laws and dynamics of materiality. The energies connected to the 4 pattern offer you an ability to persevere (or be stubborn), be loyal, and eventually find contentment working within a structure. As one very wise woman once said, "It is the banks of the river that allow the water to flow to the ocean. Without those banks, the water would never get there." I'd add, the banks help the water get there without flooding the surrounding lands. The imagination and flood of ideas emerging from the 3 need the structure of 4 to amount to something more than just hot air!

The focusing ability of the 4 pattern can become blinders to the bearer of this pattern, and that tendency should be watched, for all things are contained within a broader context which must not be overlooked. When the 4 pattern takes over to the exclusion of every other tendency, it can result in a boring companion, one so caught up in his work that he is one-sided and dull.

On the other hand, the compound 4 pattern has some very interesting aspects. The 13/4 is the number of death and rebirth, also the number of the Goddess from whose womb the fetus dies in order to be reborn as a baby into the material world. In this way the mystery of death and rebirth is present when a person's Life Path is the 13/4. Ask yourself, what needs to die in your life so that you can live more fully?

The Master Number 22 is another compound number, becoming the single digit 4 and signifies the enlightened person who brings his or her vision down to earth, embodying it in matter on a global scale. Living up to the potential in this number is quite demanding, with a danger of delusion lying within it. You are not already this all powerful person until you've done all your homework and have fulfilled the necessary requirements to channel this kind of power. Power trips or despair await a deluded 22.

The 4 Life Path is successful when it learns to apply its practical, organizational, trustworthy potential to a specific task. Working with materials such as earth, wood and metal is deeply satisfying to this hardworking pattern. By handling these materials, the laws of the physical universe are being learned at the soul level.

5

You are here to cast aside the structures which have limited your vision of possibility. Your purpose is to venture out into the world, to take in its variety, its wonder and the exciting people, places and ideas awaiting you. Freedom to explore, to taste, touch, see and use all your senses to learn about this fantastic place called Earth, is your pathway of evolution and opportunity. During your adventures out in the world, you discover all kinds of amazing things which allow you to become the life of a party, a successful salesperson, a promoter, a tour guide, or whatever activity allows you to maintain your freedom while exploring the world. It is the use of your five senses that teaches you the properties of physicality; therefore, the 5 pattern is aptly called the *number of man* for by exploring your world, you become more human.

A word of warning, however, for the addictiveness of the five senses can become destructive and slow down your spiritual progress. This is a tightrope walk through the world, to plunge into the lessons of the five senses without being overwhelmed and trapped in them.

The extroverted energy of the 5 seeks others with whom he can communicate life experiences. To this end, he may become a writer of adventure stories, providing that doesn't require too much time alone behind the typewriter; or as a speaker or conversationalist of wondrous and lively tales. Actually the 5 can liven up any subject, making them a popular choice to invite to stuffy gatherings.

6

If you have the 6 Life Path, you have a multitude of opportunities before you. After exploring the sensual world (5) and coming to a balance and understanding of matter, you are now being asked to demonstrate your maturity and to assume responsibility for a home, a relationship, a job. More than responsibility, you are being asked to provide culture and refinement. You are a community builder, an important member of political committees and groups that help the homeless, orphans, battered women, and endangered species. Loving service and humanitarian outreach is the gift of this pattern. A patron of the arts, you have come to create artistic, nurturing environments that can heal, teach and help evolve the young of any age.

This is the Life Path of the compassionate teacher and the loving parent who instructs the young in the arts of civilization, setting before them the ideal image of what it means to be human. The pitfall for the 6, however, is the discovery that even the most ideal person is human and has to come down from the pedestal to mingle with the rest of us. There can be a feeling of betrayal, or certainly great disappointment on the part of the 6 that his or her god has clay feet.

Artistic expression is important to a 6. Dance, visual arts, and music reach into the heart and soul and draw out all that is humane and meaningful within us. Myths and symbols speak to a 6, whose communication is far more connected with the heart than with the mind, and thus religion is a natural venue for a 6 Life Path.

A 6 Life Path must beware of bigotry, narrow mindedness, judgmentalness and irresponsibility. These are the negative and denial aspects of the 6, and when you are unwilling to live up to your positive potential, you may find yourself tearing down the good in society rather than building it up.

7

Until you understand the calling of the 7 Life Path, you may find yourself a loner in the world, either driving people away with your cutting, sarcastic remarks, or becoming isolated by health conditions or location. For the pattern of the 7 may present itself as a lonely path, asking you to go inward, into the hidden places of your psyche, to discover your most deeply held truth. This inner search requires the discipline of contemplation and study, the combined powers of mind and intuition.

The energy drive of the scientist is being asked of you in this Life Path, calling forth your strong mental energy that probes, analyzes, dissects, and desires to know the core of whatever comes into the center of your scrutiny. You can be a fearsome adversary for someone less well endowed. Your level of inquiry may be the exploration of the laws making up the physical world, as an astronomer, a mathematician, or a physicist.

On the other hand, your interests may be on a metaphysical level, where you become the priest or priestess, searching deep into the heart of Life itself to find meaning and wisdom.

You need time alone to contemplate your deep thoughts and to send the laser light of your mind into your explorations.

You will yearn for your Ivory Tower where you can create your perfect world among works of art and nature. Perhaps this is why the monastery, the retreat center, the quiet laboratory have so much appeal to you. You long for a place where worldly affairs do not crowd in upon you.

To be positively alone rather than lonely allows you to move forward with strength and self determination, to discover your own knowing and in so doing become a beacon of faith for yourself and others. Let your Ivory Tower become a Lighthouse for those who are also searching for truth.

8

You are challenged to be an administrator, handling the power of decision making that affects the lives and fortunes of others. By the time you have arrived at an 8 Life Path the Creative Mind has determined you ready to manage power and direct energy, for you have mastered the physical world (Patterns 1-6) and the mental-intuitional world (Pattern 7).

However, this is not a light undertaking and contains peril for the individual functioning from the ego rather than the soul level. The more responsibility you are offered in life, the more you must rise to being an ethical and trustworthy recipient of that charge. It is a truism that the higher you climb, the farther you can fall, so it is to the advantage of an 8 Life Path to hold an awareness of the good of the whole and not be concerned only with his or her own well being.

The energy directed towards a person with an 8 Life Path is intense, demanding the discipline of the mind to successfully carry out the potential in this pattern. When the individual has been properly prepared, then she can be the corporate executive, the foundation manager, the Chief Financial Officer, the university president, for all his instincts and drives are to be the head of the organization where she can manipulate the power that makes it function. The person on an 8 Life Path who is ill-prepared to meet the tension and demands of this pattern can be driven into ill-health, erroneous decisions, mismanagement of resources, and power trips which ultimately are self defeating.

In a positive expression of this pattern, the 8 learns keen discrimination, judgment, and how to make decisions about what is productive and what needs to be culled out. She develops the courage and wisdom to make the necessary decisions, to call the shots, to see behind appearances, to know what works and what doesn't. In this respect, a positive 8 Life Path would also be a wise judge, capable of making astute decisions regarding the sentencing of criminals or the recognition of the innocent.

In determining the Personal Year, the 8 year has been named the Harvest Year. It is during this time that the individual harvests the crop of the past seven years, for good or for ill. Contemplating the process of harvesting is a very helpful means of understanding the 8 pattern. First there is the gathering of the crop—cutting the hay, picking the fruit. Then, culling the crop, separating the wheat from the chaff, throwing out the rotten apples—the process of making decisions and choices. After sorting out what needs to be saved, there is the final job of preserving the crop in some form to produce a profit. The image is not of someone sitting back on his laurels being fed grapes, but of a hard worker coupled with intelligent decision making, blending and mastering the physical and mental worlds.

9

The final single digit pattern, 9, is a mystic number because it disappears into every other number (3+9=12 and 1+2=3). It is this ubiquitous quality that characterizes the 9 Life Path—the individual who transcends his or her personal self, blending into the Greater Self. To the extent the individual is successful in transcending himself, he recognizes himself in other people, discovering the drama of their lives, understanding without judgment how and why they are the way they are. For this reason, the 9 Life Path has been called the number of Universal Love, for love is the major driving force behind the 9 pattern. The love that allows it to blend and disappear into the beloved. It is not the fiercely personal blood link love of the 6, but a transcendent love.

It is this quality of empathy, of gut knowing of the other person, that allows the 9 to live in a world of drama. Emotion drives a 9 and until it can master its emotional body, life is a series of intense ups and downs where everything, no matter how small, provides a justification for dramatizing the event.

The inner recognition that the 9 belongs to the world, causes the individual with this Life Path to desire making contact with the world. Thus the 9 may become a wanderer, a traveler, finding himself everywhere. On the other hand, organizations transcending national boundaries, universal foundations, humanitarian relief organizations, spiritual groups, would appeal to a 9 for work opportunities, where he can reach out to help others for he feels their need so deeply.

The negative 9 Life Path, still resonating with the concept of the whole, can be the most selfish of all the number patterns for it wants the whole for him/herself. This may be things or people that it accumulates and hangs onto for the sake of possession. The danger in this expression of 9 becomes the Karmic number 19 where the individual must face loss and release of everything it holds dear. In this way it learns the important spiritual lesson that we are here to support our highest potential and that of everyone and everything else by our act of releasing and not possessing. Paradoxically, the negative 9 finds its redemption in the positive 1, a more enlightened sense of Self.

Life Cycles

Life Cycles fall within the broader context of the Life Path and are studied within that context. Therefore, consider your Life Cycle pattern in relation to how it interacts with your Life Path pattern. If your Cycle is a 5 and your Life Path is a 7, the lessons of 5 are for the purpose of illuminating and giving more substance to the 7. For example, an adventure in the world should be reflected upon to discern how it helps one understand the deeper meanings in life. There are three cycles: the Developmental Cycle, the Power Cycle, and the Wisdom Cycle. Each one consists of twenty-eight to thirty-two years. However, since our life span is now going beyond 84 years the final cycle may be longer, continuing to the end of a person's life.

Meaning of Cycles

First

The *Developmental cycle* lasts from birth to the age of 28 years. During this period the person is learning, studying formally or informally, and developing the skills and powers for living. The number of the cycle indicates the particular arena for growth within which this individual will be studying.

Second

Age 28 to 56, is aptly named the *Power Cycle* for it is during this period that a person enjoys his or her greatest strength. During this period people are most apt to make their mark in the outer world. Look to the number in the Power Cycle to determine the context within which the Power will be held and see how this relates to the Life Path number and the Pinnacle.

Third

The *Wisdom Cycle* is the final cycle, for it is here that all the experiences and learning in a person's life have been garnered. From this place of knowing, people can share their knowing with others. It is also here that the energy begins to withdraw from the outer world and turn inward, deepening the integration and understanding of what one's life has been about. Look to the number pattern in this cycle to see what unfinished business still needs to be integrated into a better understanding of your life. What wisdom have you garnered that gives you dignity and peace in your final years?

Refer to your analysis chart and check the Heart Persona, and Essence numbers which matche your current age. If you have three names, a first, a middle and a last, these correspond to the first, middle and last Life Cycles. If you have only two names, consider the first name corresponding to about 45 years and the second name also 45 years. If you have four names, then each name corresponds to about 22 years. Do the active numbers from your name support the forces operative in your Life Path? Consider how you could integrate and organize the various patterns found in these positions. This is where the art of Numerology comes into play.

Cycle Descriptions

1

Above all, during this cycle develop the courage to stand on your own, think independently, and come to a greater degree of self knowledge. Apply your resourcefulness and individuality towards furthering your Life Path.

2

A need to work cooperatively and in partnership with others is called for in this cycle. Be sensitive to others, supportive of their needs and handle the details in your life.

3

Bring joy and companionship into your environment. Learn to play with others, to enjoy sharing your stories, jokes, and music. Whatever your Life Path pattern is, bring lightness into the equation and don't take yourself too seriously.

4

Your loyalty and perseverence will be called upon in this cycle. You will need to work hard, be organized, stay focused and construct the foundation for the task of your Life Path.

5

A need to learn more about the natural world and apply this knowledge to your Life Path is being requested of you. To become fully human you need to understand and be acquainted with the physical world; this cycle is your opportunity to tackle that challenge.

6

Whatever your Life Path pattern is about, during this cycle you need to accept responsibility for it, be generous and nurture the relationships that come into your life. You may find yourself actively involved in the arts or community service.

7

You are being offered 28 years to dig deeply and uncover the truth about your Life Path pattern. You may have gone into this period with doubts and fears, but if you apply yourself to the 7 pattern, you will discover your core of belief and overcome your fears.

8

An opportunity to understand power and choice has come up for you during this cycle. Your Life Path pattern will benefit by furthering your education, administrating good judgment, and being willing to take leadership whenever offered to you..

9

During this 28 year period you will learn how to transcend your own needs in order to be responsive to the needs of a greater whole, perhaps family, community, nation. This is a cycle to practice forgiveness, to complete projects, and to empty out your personal life. A full cup is unable to receive new experiences. The drama of life may be quite poignant during this cycle.

Pinnacles

Pinnacles represent periods in our lives when we are presented with key learning experiences. Your pinnacle numbers will help you identify the lessons and skills you are intended to extract from these experiences. The first Pinnacle can last from 27 to 34 years, and therefore it is of exceeding importance that you become fully acquainted with the pattern offered. Denying or rejecting it means you carry the burden of this unresolved, unlearned pattern throughout your life where it can hold you back from the potential that should rightly be yours.

To review how to obtain your Pinnacle numbers, refer to page 59. The length of the first Pinnacle is determined by your Life Path number subtracted from the age of 36. Therefore, if your Life Path is a 1, your first Pinnacle will end at age 35. However, if your Life Path is a 9, your first Pinnacle will end at age 27.

Once the first Pinnacle has been completed, the second and third pinnacles last a period of nine years each. The final and fourth Pinnacle will last until your final transition.

A brief description of the Pinnacles is given below. For a more complete understanding of the pinnacle number pattern, refer to Section II, Uncovering the Number Patterns.

Pinnacle Descriptions

1

You must become self-directed and have a sound understanding of who you are. Then drawing from this knowledge of yourself, be willing to initiate projects, step into the unknown, and use your creative abilities towards furthering your Life Path demands.

2

Learn to cooperate and make peace between varying points of view. Be attentive to details and find balance in your life. This requires you to develop your sensitivity and ability to communicate clearly and compassionately.

3

Draw out your inner child and rejoice in its ability to imagine, to spin flights of fancy, and its love of play and fun. You need to lighten up, which is the first step towards enlightenment. Express yourself in words and art and, when you do, unleash your restraints in the spirit of joy.

4

You must learn to organize yourself, to develop structures for your ideas, and stay with them until they have been accomplished. Apply yourself, even if the work seems like drudgery, because this ability to persevere is what you need to successfully fulfill your Life Path.

5

During a Pinnacle of 5 you are being challenged to become free, to release old structures that no longer serve your life progress and to expose yourself to new ideas, new groups of people, new places that can expand your outlook. You are being challenged to no longer cling to comfort and safety but to strike out and risk in order to grow.

6

Responsibility and service are the name of the game when you have a 6 Pinnacle. You are being asked to understand and be responsive to relationships, your life companion, children, students, parents. Planning for the highest and best good of your community is a worthy activity during a 6 Pinnacle.

7

This is a time for reflection, inner contemplation, searching out the primary questions of meaning and origin. You need to guard yourself during this period, to hold off the confusion and chaos of the outer world, allowing yourself the peace and space within which you can do your inner work. This does not mean you need to remove yourself from the world, only that you must be true to yourself and find periods of uninterrupted quiet.

8

You are being asked to strengthen and apply your own inner authority to handle the events that enter your life. Make sound judgments, face up to decisions, find your power and do not be afraid to assert it providing you discern that the situation is appropriate. Take classes in management, in assertiveness training, or whatever will strengthen your mind, your understanding, and thus your ability to be a leader. You have the opportunity to achieve fame and wealth during this Pinnacle.

9

Your opportunity to learn personal transcendence is within the 9 Pinnacle. Release your ego demands, your need to own and possess, and attune to the good of the whole. Discover the stories and dramas within others, walk in their shoes for a bit, see through their eyes. Find the commonalities present in all people and cultures.

Hidden Life Path Number (HLP)

Juggling all the information about your Life Path, with all its various aspects, can be a challenge. Even so, it is crucially important to understand the individual patterns presented by your Life Path, Cycle and Pinnacle numbers. What important insights and lessons do they provide? What is the essence of these various patterns as they interact with each other? These interactions constitute a "hidden quality" that can unveil valuable keys about your life. You will need to determine your Hidden Life Path Number to determine what this quality is.

No other numerology book that I know of reveals this number. Over my years of working with numerology, the extraction of the HLP number from the chart came from an obvious extension of numerological principles.

The value of the HLP number has been shown over and over again when working with it on clients' charts, providing insights which are not obtained in other ways. In my own chart I discovered this HLP number was identical to my first Pinnacle. Reflecting on my own personal history, I know how poorly I handled that period in my life. I am also aware that I am in the midst of an intensive *relearning* of the positive aspects of this number pattern right now. As the HLP pattern does not show up in the overt aspects of my chart, discovering how to reveal it has given this period of my life more significance.

A simple way to discover this hidden quality is to add your Life Path and current Cycle and Pinnacle together. Reduce the sum to a single digit, while retaining any Master or Karmic information. This final number is the key to your specific and current learning assignment.

Refer to the Life Path descriptions at the beginning of this section to understand the application of this pattern to you. The number pattern you come up with may be that of a previous Cycle or Pinnacle which was not completed, or one of your challenge positions. Study your chart to determine in what way your Hidden Life Path number pattern is helping you evolve right now.

As an example, I have chosen a real life person with a 5 Life Path, who is in a 3 Life Cycle and an 8 Life Pinnacle. The summation of the Hidden Life Path is therefore a 16/7 (5+3+8=16/7). Review the information on the karmic number 16 which speaks of loss of love. She is in the process of divorcing her husband and looking deeply into the meaning of her life. She has returned to her birth name which offers the tools that she needs right now for success. Neither the Life Path, the Cycle nor the Pinnacle alone would have pointed to the intensity of her present search for answers to her life, yet the 16/7 HLP gives her insight into what this period is all about and how the pain of it can be transformed into positive learning.

VI

BUMPY ROAD AHEAD: THE SHADOW AND PROJECTION

Introduction

The psychologist, Carl Jung, contributed a vast body of knowledge to our understanding of the human psyche. Among many worthwhile concepts, he gave us the concept of a Shadow self and the mechanism known as Projection. These concepts are so useful to our interpretation of the Numerology Chart that in order to derive the full implication of these two important positions, the Table of Soul Quality Development and the Challenge Position, I am going to discuss briefly the significance of these psychological phenomena.

The Shadow, no relationship to the radio and movie personality of Lamont Cranston, describes the unacknowledged and repressed parts of our self. Although when Cranston says in his guise as the Shadow, "Who knows what evil lurks in the hearts of men? The Shadow knows," he certainly hints at the truth. These Shadow elements are those parts of ourselves that we'd rather not acknowledge. We deny to ourselves that we have these unwanted qualities and can be quite successful at hiding the truth of their existence from ourselves. We may not even know we have these qualities even though they may be enormously strong forces in our lives.

How could it happen that these traits have disappeared from our awareness? Think back to the totally natural behavior of a little child who has not yet been saddled with an artificial system of behavior in order to satisfy the *shoulds* and *should nots* of parents, and later of teachers and peers. A child does something unacceptable to these authority figures and is punished. "This is bad, a no-no," they will say. Eventually the message gets through and the child pushes these behaviors back into the dark recesses of its subconsciousness. But that doesn't necessarily mean they have gone away; they've just been shoved out of sight where they continue to act out their typical behavior. Now, however, this behavior is not innocent, it has become sneaky, often vindictive and hostile, and lashes out at the world in such a way that the personality, or ego, can say, with total, wide-eyed innocence, "I didn't do it! It's the other guy over there that did it!"

That last statement, "....it's the other guy that did it," is called *projection.* We project our unacceptable and unacknowledged parts as individuals, families, groups and nations. And if the concept of extraterrestrials takes hold in the world, we will be projecting all the bad stuff onto them. We already are doing this in science fiction movies.

This denial and unwillingness to take responsibility for our *whole* self is at the root of most illness and dis-ease in our physical-mental-emotional bodies and in our world. It's imperative for healing ourselves that we courageously pull back the shutters and take a look at our Shadow—bring it out into the light. This can be terribly painful, requiring a good deal of personal honesty instead of denying what is in us. But if we can accomplish this heroic feat, we will truly transform the dragon within into a tremendously powerful ally, for believe it or not, the Shadow has within it the storehouse of our life energy. When we are able to transform the Shadow into an ally we gain a part of ourselves we didn't have before and it will help us make our journeys a resounding success instead of a whimpering effort.

An interesting twist to the Shadow is that it isn't necessarily just bad stuff that is being denied. We may have such a low opinion of ourselves that we cannot accept the good in us, and so this is what is projected onto others. Outside of ourselves are the good people, the beautiful people, the smart people. We can't quite acknowledge our own goodness and beauty and intelligence. Just imagine how much better this world could be if, instead of our denying our goodness and projecting it onto others unrealistically, we could bring these constructive and positive traits into our conscious self and start to act in a positive and powerful way in our world. Now we can act out of our strength instead of being powerless and fearful. Also, have you noticed how often your heros fall off their pedestals? This is not because they are bad, but because your Shadow was projecting totally unrealistic expectations onto them.

Spend some time contemplating your Shadow and what it projects onto the world around you. This knowledge can liberate you in ways you cannot even imagine. Moreover, these principles can explain much of the grief and violence we experience in our world.

The Table of Soul Qualities Development

This Table rightfully belongs with the analysis of the name. However, I have put it in this special section with the challenges to emphasize our need in understanding the role of the Shadow in our lives. In assigning numbers to the letters in your name, you may have discovered some numbers missing from your name. Where a number was missing, you put a zero beside that number. We call these the area of the Shadow self.

Why are the number patterns missing? One possibility is that in a past life you were unable or unwilling to work with the demands of these patterns. Because you are here to evolve, you came into this life with your Soul eager to balance out this part of your life (your chart). You may discover that you have projected these missing patterns onto other people, particularly those closest to you. You may unconsciously seek out the missing qualities in others in an effort to create your own wholeness. This has its virtues in that you may find models of behavior to emulate. But there's also the danger that you will see yourself as incapable of having these virtues for yourself. Let it be said, from one who knows from personal experience, that you will never find your wholeness outside of yourself!

Before leaping in and saying, "But it's impossible that I'm missing the 8 or 4, etc., because, if anything, I'm stronger in (the missing number[s]) than anything else." Think about it. Do we identify ourselves more with our totally accepted attributes or with those parts of ourselves with which we have struggled and finally mastered? Remember, your Table of Soul Qualities Development indicates what you were born with, not with what you have developed over the years. In reading charts, I have often noticed a person with a missing number has that number in one of the birth date positions of Cycle or Pinnacle, or perhaps in the Heart's Desire position.

This is a strong message that our souls put a high priority on accepting opportunities and challenges to learn, integrate, and demonstrate the missing number patterns.

On the other hand, a number pattern with more than three letters in the name (with the exception of the 5 which I will explain below) creates a situation of over-compensation. What I mean by this is that too much of a good thing can sometimes result in the use of that pattern like a sledge hammer. We all love a child, but if an adult behaves in a totally immature and inappropriate fashion, we don't love that even though their behavior might be very similar to their toddler counterpart. We consider that person a bore, a *puer* or *puela,* a fool.

The number pattern of 5 is an exception to the rule and this is because the 5 is known as the number of Humanity. The soul, entering into a three dimensional world, must gather all the experience this world has to offer. The pattern of gathering physical information is the primary function of the 5, for the five senses are equipped to explore and understand physical/material existence. But even this gathering of physical information can be carried to an extreme, resulting in a very unstable and grossly sensual person. More than five 5's is flirting with more restlessness and sensationalism than may be necessary or comfortable for a balanced life.

Below you will find brief explanations about the Table of Soul Quality Development. Refer to Section II, Uncovering the Number Patterns, and the list of denial and excess descriptions for each number pattern for further clarification.

Meanings
For Table of Soul Quality Development

1

Denial

In your past life you had an unwillingness to confront issues with determination and resolve. You were indecisive, looking to others for authority and leadership. You probably procrastinated on new projects and looked to others to rescue you.

You may have to struggle in this life in order to discover your own strength of the 1 pattern before you can assert your own individuality and courage.

Excess

You attempted to dominate all situations, particularly other people, insisting things go your way. You had a tenancy to be egocentric and arrogant.

In this life, you may find love eluding you until you learn to identify and be compassionate with others.

2

Denial

You were undiplomatic, even rude and insensitive to the needs and feelings of others. Details bothered you, such as keeping appointments on time, or replenishing the larder. You avoided accountability.

Life may have many opportunities in store for you to learn patience and consideration of others and attention to details.

Excess

Your motto was to keep peace at any cost, to the extent that justice was not served, and denial became a way of life. You became so lost in the details of things that you missed the forest for the trees.

Your true sense of finding balance and justice will be mastered as you find your inner courage to stand for truth and hang onto your own personal identity.

3

Denial

When opportunities to speak your piece came your way, you hid in the background, unwilling to be seen or heard. Joy and spontaneity were lacking in your life, while your powers of imagination went untapped.

This life you need to force yourself to come out from behind your mother's skirts, to speak and lecture, and draw upon those wondrous qualities of the Inner Child. In this way you learn to honor the 3 pattern.

Excess

Self expression, particularly in talking, made you a bore. Your fantasy ran wild and a healthy spontaneity was carried to the extreme of imprudent impulsiveness. You scattered your creative energy and ended up accomplishing nothing.

Find a medium to contain all of those words and fantasies, perhaps a journal or another form of creative writing, and by placing outside of yourself the excess energy of expression you will find the truth and beauty of your inner wisdom and learn how best to tell your story or create your work of art.

4

Denial

Laziness and slovenly behavior created a life of victimization and failure. Your resolve to stand true to your convictions crumbled in face of hardship and the need for endurance.

The need to work hard to accomplish the success you strive for will be a major part of your life experience until you have mastered the ability to endure and persevere in the face of physical challenges.

Excess

In a past life you became obsessed with hard work to the point where you had tunnel vision, unable to respond to anything except work.

Life will have a way of prying you out of your comfortable niche and thrusting you into the world, perhaps moving you around so often you are unable to put down roots.

5

Denial

You avoided life experiences in the past, particularly those including the great diversity of other people and the myriad possibilities of nature. When opportunities came to you for change, you would turn them down, preferring to stay in your secure and safe place.

Your success this life will depend upon your ability to flow with change and embrace the multitudinous facets of this physical world. Keep your bag packed and ready to go!

Excess

You loved the world too much--that is, the physical aspects of the world. Your zest for travel, for new places, new sights, and sensual and sexual indulgences, caused you to be shiftless and unable to be responsible.

Life experiences will curb your restlessness and impatience, teaching you to balance these physical hungers by a need to accept responsibility and to be grounded. Your success comes as you accept this balancing act.

6

Denial

You shirked responsibility in a past life, refusing to make commitments and not wanting to be tied down. Rather than discovering the beauty of service, you preferred to look the other way. Your early home life was disrupted in some way so that you were denied the model which could prepare you for creating your own happy home.

For your success this lifetime, you must accept the responsibilities and commitments that come your way and not reject them. Learn to uncover the joys and blessings to be found in service to others.

Excess

You were overbearing and burdened those around you with smothering love, running the lives of those closest to you by deciding for them what they should be and do. By being so possessive and jealous, you denied them the opportunity to fulfill their own life path.

Until you have mastered your ability to offer love freely with no strings attached, you will continually feel denied of the love you so desire. Love yourself, develop your own full potential, and you will find yourself able to offer this gift to others.

7

Denial

You refused to look inward to your own inner strength and wisdom in a past life, resulting in a state of fearfulness as the world seemed so out of control. When experiences presented themselves to you for deeper analysis and examination, you were intellectually lazy and chose rather to go along with the crowd.

Life may put you in a setting where you are forced to depend upon yourself for companionship and answers. Your freedom from fear will come about as you discover the Teacher Within, and develop your faith in life's ultimate blueprint for your own spiritual unfoldment.

Excess

Your zeal for intellectual dissection and spiritual or scientific probing caused you to become isolated in your Ivory Tower until you could no longer identify with the rest of humanity. Your sense of compassion suffered as a result and you became critical, sarcastic, and aloof.

Knowing the inner truths is a wonderful search, but keep in mind what this search is all about. Each one of us is a member of a greater body, and our individual attainment contributes to the hologram of humanity. Your elitist attitude will be knocked down to one of humility and commonality as you discover the wisdom in so-called ordinary people.

8

Denial

When opportunities to take charge, to use your powers of judgment, and to direct the activities of others came to you in a past life, you rejected these, choosing rather to live your own individual and personal life. You scorned managing your finances, perhaps believing this was beneath you or somehow dirty.

Life experiences will be presented to you where your success depends upon your taking control and managing your finances and the activities of others. You will need to acquire as much educational information and experience as you can in order to discharge your opportunities with wisdom and knowledge.

Excess
Your zest for taking over the role of management and authority went a bit too far in a past life. You became a sort of Napoleon character. Your love of power impinged upon the rights of others.

Life may put you into a position of subservience for awhile as you learn the important lesson that before you can rule, you must learn to serve. Once your 8 pattern has been balanced out, you can then resume your natural gifts for management.

As you may have noticed when studying the excess of any number, the antidote for the excess is reaching to acquire and master the next number pattern. Therefore, as an example, a too zealous 6 pattern must go within the 7 pattern to find the strength and comfort of the inner self, rather than looking always to loved ones to satisfy that craving for relationship. Or an excessive, dominating 1 pattern, who walks all over the rights and feelings of others, must reach for the 2 pattern of receptivity and sensitivity to the people around him or her.

Challenges

Another position on the Numerology Chart, located within the Life Path section or the birth date, describes the challenges along your journey through life. These share many of the characteristics of the Soul Quality Development table, and are another aspect of the Shadow. The difference lies in their origin.

The Soul Quality Development characteristics result in the denial or excessive expression of the pattern in a past life, whereas the Challenge position represents characteristics which are a part of your present life but are repressed or otherwise hidden in your subconsciousness. Your Life Path experiences challenge you to draw up these repressed attributes into your consciousness. By acknowledging you have this fund of ability within you and by using it, you become so much stronger and more resourceful at solving the problems set before you.

Please refer to your chart as you developed it in Section III. Under the date of your birth there are four Challenge positions, corresponding with the four Pinnacle positions which are indicated above the birth date. The age when you move from one Challenge to the next is the same age that you move from one Pinnacle to the next. However, the third Challenge position is your Main Challenge which resonates through your whole life. If a Challenge number shows up more than once, and this is often the case, that Challenge is more severe, requiring more effort on your part to overcome its negative influence in your life.

Below is a brief description of the various Challenges. For a more complete understanding of the Challenge and the potential available to you if you use this pattern consciously, refer to Section II, Uncovering the Number Patterns. Use the Number Affirmations to integrate the pattern with your conscious self. As you read the Challenges below, preface by saying to yourself, *"I have an abundance of [this number pattern] in me, and I claim it now."*

1

Challenge
I may be domineering, rude, selfish, egotistical, and demanding, a go-it-alone person without concern for others.

Affirmation
I have the ability to be inventive, creative, and individualistic and am able to find new ways to achieve my goals, being both assertive and courageous in the process while remaining alert to the needs of others.

2

Challenge
I may be co-dependent, clingy, self-effacing, with low self-esteem. I may also be insensitive, blame others and deny my psychic ability.

Affirmation
I have the ability to handle details, be sensitive to others and find the diplomatic solutions which result in fairness and peace. I like myself.

3

Challenge
I may be too shy, not speak up, squelch my artistic expression, or imagine everyone hates me.

Affirmation
I have the ability to express myself spontaneously and artistically, bringing joy and delight into the lives of others.

4

Challenge
I may be slovenly, undisciplined and disorganized, unwilling to carry my share of work.

Affirmation
I have the ability to build solid foundations, to organize materials and work hard. I have a strong sense of truth and loyalty.

5

Challenge
I may hold back from new experiences in fear, or be addicted to sexual and sensual experiences. My restlessness interferes with and prevents me from accomplishing my goals.

Affirmation
I have the ability to embrace change and life experiences, to mingle with all kinds of people and gather new ideas. I share my adventures with others.

6

Challenge
I may be unresponsive to the needs around me and unwilling to help others. I could interfere with the destiny of another and

attempt to control their life. I may be bigoted, judgmental and opinionated.

Affirmation
I have the ability to handle responsibility while serving others lovingly. I can create artistic and nurturing environments.

7

Challenge
I can be anti-social, too analytical, not willing to know myself, or conversely, surfing through life, unwilling to probe deeply for the truth of a situation. I may be a perfectionist to the extreme, nit-picking and finding fault with others.

Affirmation
I have the ability to search out the inner truth, to analyze and to know. My knowing brings me the wisdom and the ability to overcome my fears.

8

Challenge
I may be unmindful of properly overseeing my physical world, including my finances and property, and may make poor judgments about people and circumstances.

Affirmation
I have the ability to manage, to discriminate, to judge and to handle power masterfully. I can truly deliver the goods.

0

Challenge

All the number patterns may be my challenge, with no one of them more outstanding than any other. I have arrived at the place in my soul evolution where I can handle all challenges.

Affirmation

I have the ability to choose, to accept the possibility that I can bring forward all my strengths to meet the challenge set before me.

VII

YOUR DESTINATION AND
YOUR JOURNEY THROUGH TIME

Introduction

During our lifetimes we are subjected to new influences, such as name changes and new cycles, both on a universal and personal scale. All of this occurs in the natural course of growth which takes place as we struggle or cooperate with our life lessons. Although our natal chart provides the basis for looking at the influences affecting us, none of us remains fixed in the same consciousness with which we were born. We make choices in our lives and these choices support our spiritual growth, or get us locked into the prisons of self-limitation which come when we consistently choose the negative expressions of our numbers.

By analyzing the name we are currently using, we discover what vibrational patterns we are drawing to ourselves in this specific period of time. Are these in harmony with our original name, or in conflict? Does this name offer us some of the missing number patterns from our original name, helping us to acquire and strengthen those missing aspects of ourselves? What position(s) on our charts is being helped by our new name and what part is in conflict?

In this section we look primarily at the Power Goal, the Universal and Personal Years, which tell us what vibrational patterns are currently active in our lives.

Power Goal

Around the age of 36, a new influence begins to emerge in your life. As you grow older, this influence becomes stronger and more pervasive. By the time you retire, if you choose to retire, this influence, called the Power Goal, will be your way of making your mark on the world before you make your big transition into the next life. Often this Pattern is exactly what you want, your present from Spirit for living a good life. However, if your life has been one of denial and not doing what you came to do, then the Power Goal can slip through your fingers.

Briefly, the Power Goal is what your life has been aiming towards. It is the integration of who you can be as you acquire new abilities learned upon your Life Path. In other words, your Power Goal is the fulfillment of the person you have come to be.

You acquire the Power Goal Number by adding together the Essence number (the combination of vowels and consonants) and the Life Path number. The sum is your Power Goal Pattern. Think of it as the icing on the cake, the dessert at the end of the meal and allow the most positive expression of the number pattern define what your Power Goal will be. Below are samples of Power Goals:

POWER GOALS

1

Your goal has brought you to a sense of unity, of individualistic focus and leadership. You know who you are and you can assert this knowledge in your life with courage, determination and self-assurance.

2

You have become cooperative, a peacemaker, a diplomat, a person sensitive to others. You nurture and support others and are in caring partnership with others. Your psychic abilities are finely tuned.

3

You can express yourself easily and spontaneously for the pleasure and enjoyment of others. You have made peace with your inner child and can play with creative joy. You may have successfully written your book, or are in the process of doing so, performed your art and entertained others.

4

You experience the admiration of others for the outstanding loyalty and trustworthiness you have exhibited in your life. Your ability to bring order out of chaos, your faithfulness and loyalty, and your willingness to dig in and work hard, find an appreciative audience. Through your work you have helped to lay the foundation for succeeding generations.

5

You have enlivened the world with your spirit of adventure and excitement in all aspects of material existence. Because of this curiosity about nature and your extroverted ways, you have helped others become more conscious and appreciative of the world in which they live.

6

Even though your children are now grown up and on their own, your influence in their lives and in the life of the community carries on. You have helped to create the organizations and vehicles that perpetuate culture and civilization. Your work with people less fortunate wins you admiration and praise.

7

After years of searching, you have found your inner truth and the faith that allows you to banish fear in your own life and in those who are touched by your deep knowing. You have gone to the depths in whatever arena which has appealed to you, and can thus provide a map of this inner world to guide the lives of others.

8

Your keen sense of administration and authority allow you to retain your power and judgment into your final years. You have acquired many of the good things in life—fame, fortune and possessions—through your keen discrimination, your judgment and your astute leadership.

9

You have earned the right to transcend yourself and merge with God, or whatever that Great Spirit means to you. You find yourself able to release the shackles of the ego and find a pure love for your fellow man and for yourself. To the end, you will find yourself enraptured by the drama of life

Universal and Personal Years

We grow and develop in cycles. Some systems use the seven year cycle; this system of numerology works with the nine year cycle. These cycles affect our personal lives as well as the evolutionary development of the Earth. They are based upon the current calendar, and one can only suppose they work because over the past many hundreds of years we have come to accept the dating of the calendar and put that belief into the Collective Unconscious Mind. Otherwise, why would it work? Our calendar is certainly not using the same dating as the Pythagorean calendar. I am not offering this book of numerology as a hard science, only giving information that has been useful in the lives of many people. It may also be useful for you. It has certainly worked for me.

With these considerations in mind, the Universal Year is determined by the formula given on page 61. We look at what is happening on a broad global scale when considering the Universal Year. It is noteworthy that in November of 1998 the President of the United States was impeached—the first impeachment of well-over one hundred years and the second in the history of the nation. This event was an ending to the Presidency as we have known it, coming on a 9 Universal Year.

There were dire prophesies from many sources for the year 1998 which did not affect all of us living on this planet. On the other hand there were millions of people around the globe whose lives were severely affected in that year by El Niño, earthquakes in Italy, fires consuming the rainforests in Brazil and Indonesia, devastating hurricanes in Latin America, whales beaching themselves in New Zealand, war in Bosnia and Turkey, and ever-present starvation in Africa. Surely, something is coming to an end and a new beginning is sorely needed.

1999,which adds up to a 1 Universal Year, is the time for sowing seeds which will begin to emerge in the year 2001, a 3 year. Could it be that the revelation of our President's sex life will determine the elections in the year 2000? The newly elected president is installed into office in the year 2001!

Our Personal Year normally begins in January; however, there is much controversy over this timing, particularly for people born in the latter part of the year. A compromise is to consider the year having twelve months and the birth date coming right during the middle of that period. Therefore, if the birthday is in March, the Personal Year will begin to show itself in September of the previous year. With our example, that would be in September of 1998, coming to its peak in March of 1999, terminating around the end of August of the same year.

The best way to determine when your Personal Year starts for you is to become familiar with what happens to you during the nine year cycle: What is your sense of a shift occurring from one pattern to another? When do you sow seeds? When do you harvest? This is not a perfect system but one which is useful in organizing what can be chaotic experiences.

Our Personal Year is far more compelling to us than the Universal Year unless we are working in areas that reach beyond our personal lives, such as business, industry, sales, politics, and so forth. It is then useful to look at the universal picture to see how our personal cycle fits into the overall cycle.

Are we supported by the Universal Year, or does it neutralize our personal cycle? Or perhaps we are at odds with it. If the Universal Year is a 5 where changes are occurring on a global scale, and we are in our 4 Personal Year, we may find ourselves unable to go with the flow, so consumed with organizing our own lives that we miss some of the bigger opportunities. On the other hand, if the Universal Year is a 1 and our Personal Year is also a 1, we are right in line with the universal vibrations and can use that *universal* support during our nine year cycle.

Sequential numbers are at odds with each other (i.e., 1-2, 3-4, etc.); however, if the numbers of the Universal Year are even numbers, and our Personal Year also is an even number, we are in harmony with the Universal Year and can benefit accordingly. The same principle holds true with odd numbers on both Universal and Personal Years.

127

Year 1

A time for new beginnings—planting seeds for new projects, relationships, moving to a new location, starting a class or new career, or just beginning to mull over a new idea. Sometimes these new beginnings are almost invisible to us or they may seem insignificant. Their importance, however, begins to be disclosed in subsequent years.

Year 2

A year in which the new seed germinates, begins to send down roots, tastes the soil around it, and at last takes hold. But it is still underground and needs nurturing and care. Don't expect much from it at this time.

Year 3

This is a year to celebrate the first outward appearance of the new growth. A flood of ideas and possibilities may inundate you this year, and your imagination can run rampant. But overall, it's a year to enjoy and to play.

Year 4

A year to organize yourself. It is sometimes called the Survival of the Fittest Year, for this is a time to apply yourself diligently if you want your new growth to bear fruit.

Year 5

A year to gather more information and develop social contacts, to promote your project with others, talk about it, develop a marketing plan to sell it, and to find what refinements and possibilities could be added to it.

Year 6

A year to face up to your relationships, perhaps to bring new loves into your life or decide to part from old loves. A year to take responsibility for your project, work on its packaging, see how it can benefit others or enhance the field of art.

Year 7

A year to gain important insight into what your project is really all about. You need to spend time alone reflecting on what you are doing and why you are doing it. A year to be alone but not lonely, to analyze yourself, your life and your work. A year to develop more faith in yourself.

Year 8

A year to reap the harvest of your project, planted seven years earlier. This is a time to make decisions about what is of value and needs to be preserved, or what you want to cull out. It is a year to plan how to finance your project and how you want to work with others.

Year 9

You've worked and played with your project for eight years and now is the time to send it out into the world, tie up all your loose ends and prepare yourself to begin a new cycle.

VIII

MAKING YOUR CHART
COME ALIVE

Integrating Your Chart

During the course of this book you have compared one position with another position to see how these relate with each other. As you become familiar with the Numerology chart, doing your own, then those of your family and friends, the numbers will begin to come alive for you, playing out their interactive dance. Use your growing awareness of the numbers to hone your skills at weaving the components of the chart together.

It can be useful to think of the chart as a play. The name describes the actor who has been given the starring role. Each actor has his own passions, strengths and talents to bring to the play. The Life Path is the name of the drama he has come to act out. We have seen many Hamlets over the years, and each one is different because of the personality and intention of the actor. A drama such as Hamlet usually has three acts, which are the Cycles. Within the acts are scenes, the Pinnacles, each one highlighting some of the action which contributes to the drama of the play as a whole.

Example 1.

"You mean it's okay for me to write and it's not escaping responsibility after all?" my client asked. I was explaining to her that the purpose and mission she came to express was that imaginative, creative side of herself. "I've always wanted to write but felt that I needed to be a supportive person and help other people, and that it was selfish of me to spend my time writing for my own pleasure," she said.

We had looked at her chart which was over balanced in the 6 pattern (6 Heart's Desire, 6 Persona, 6 Life Path, 6 Cornerstone). The 6, of course, has to do with taking responsibility, nurturing and serving others and being a good parent. These were tasks she had performed all her life, sometimes cheerfully and willingly, other times feeling trapped and suffocated by the needs of others who demanded her time and attention. Yet, in the position of her life purpose, which is the Essence number, the summation of vowels and consonants, describing why she was here in this particular body and time, the pattern of 3 appeared. From our study of the number patterns, we know the 3 denotes the imaginative, expressive child which is the very opposite expression from that of the parent. The Inner Child of this woman was outclassed by so much parental energy. As so often happens when an aspect of our lives is suppressed, it surfaces in its negative form, and this client, who had a strong drive to express her Inner Child, but had been caught up in the outer demand to perform responsibly, often found it difficult to be as reliable as the task demanded. Instead, she escaped into fiction and fantasy, neglecting the work at hand. The Inner Child would sabotage relationships she attempted to form, or responsibilities she would take on.

What her chart suggested was that her parenting drive, which was strongly indicated in the many positions on her chart, needed also to be directed towards supporting and encouraging her own inner child, enabling it to express the inner creativity so central to her essence. Surely, this ability to see the world with the eyes of a child, to be spontaneous and joyous, this *incredible lightness of being*, is every bit as important to Life as being responsible and faithful to duty. Neither one offers a complete pattern, but balanced with each other, they beautifully contribute to the health, of both the society and the individual.

This client, now reassured that she wasn't shirking her *duty* by writing, and receiving the empowerment of her numerology chart, began to channel her energies into writing stories and books.

Example 2

This client had two 3's in her name and her Essence was a 3 pattern, nevertheless her main Challenge was also a 3 which she experienced as a fear of expressing herself in words. We talked about this puzzle in an attempt to understand its deeper meaning. In the course of our conversation, she told me a very interesting story. During her life she has been an interpreter for the hearing impaired and became an expert with sign language—a silent form of expression. She had recently had a past life reading in which she saw herself as an interpreter for Native Americans who were negotiating a peace treaty. This was not a consensual desire on the parts of the tribes involved and she was strangled and killed for her efforts at making peace.

The throat is the energy center for speaking and expression, which would indicate a fear of speaking out; after all, she was killed for doing just that. So her Numerology chart showed her strength in speaking and expression, that is, her natural impulse to express herself. But because of her hidden fear, she felt a need to express herself silently (signing) and was verbally repressed. Understanding why she was repressed, despite her natural inclination to speak, has helped her reinforce her Life's Mission (her 3 Essence).

Example 3

All indications on my client's chart, with the exception of the Heart's Desire and the Cornerstone positions, were mental/spiritually inclined. She is a woman who is on a sincere spiritual path, devoting herself full time to this pursuit. And yet the passion that drives her, indicated by the 4 Heart's Desire, seemed out of keeping with its material emphasis. I felt uncertain about it until she told me how important structure was in her life and that her spiritual pursuits needed to be grounded. She is active in body work and healing which is a fine blending of the physical/material 4 pattern and the 7 Essence and the 9 Life Path. Also, her passion in life, the activity that keeps her balanced, is growing plants, both for food and beauty.

IX

COMPANIONS ON THE PATH

Relationships

Have you ever wondered why you are drawn to a particular person or life partner? You might have asked, what is the reason for my being with this person? What can we learn from each other? What can we create together? Numerology can offer clues as to why we are attracted to certain people, what we might hope to accomplish with them, and what lessons we have to teach each other.

We are often drawn to certain people for their strength in areas in which we are weak. Their wisdom and experience can teach us and help us to grow, providing we avoid the pitfall of being lazy and letting them carry the quality in which we are weak. Rejecting the opportunity to develop the strengths of our partner may result in creating a marriage of extremes–each of us at the opposite end of the spectrum. Perhaps you have noticed how one partner in a marriage can be so gracious whereas the other one is contemptible. Or how one may take responsibility for all the details of running a household while the other partner seems utterly dependent on the other person for basic needs such as preparing meals or doing laundry. Wouldn't it be preferable to achieve a more wholesome balance in the relationship by developing the needed qualities from the other person? This is not to say we can't delegate tasks and so divide up the work. Nor does it necessarily mean that you will become as good at doing everything your partner does well. But becoming aware of what attracts us to each other, and how this attraction appears to be a way to make our lives whole is important. Start this exploration by looking at where your chart indicates weakness, and then at the chart of your friend, and see where you each may be strong or weak in relation to the other.

To clarify this point with an example, let us consider the case of a married couple. Jane's chart has five 1's and no 2's whereas her partner Joe's chart has four 1's and three 2's. Jane's chart shows she has a great deal of self assertion and self confidence but lacks that quality of sensitivity and receptivity to another person's ideas personified by the number pattern of 2. This lack in her may have created difficulties for her in her life. She is attracted to Joe, who not only is able to be strongly independent (the four 1's), but also has the capacity to see the point of view of not just himself, but of others, and create a climate of understanding and negotiation (the three 2's). Joe's strength in the 2 vibration may be what Jane's soul is needing to bring about a greater sense of wholeness; therefore Jane associates with Joe, learning about peacemaking either through example or by his gentle guidance into understanding this quality of the 2.

Before jumping to conclusions, however, look at the chart as a whole. Someone may not have brought their 2 with them in the Table of Soul Quality Development, but may have the 2 represented in the Soul line (the vowels above the name). Also, in constructing many charts, I have discovered that the missing vibration from the Table of Soul Quality Development often shows up in the Life Path, Cycles, or Pinnacles. This is an indication the Soul definitely wishes to master the missing vibration and the individual may be strongly drawn to someone who has that vibration in a major position or an abundance of this vibration in his or her chart.

Another magnetic factor between individuals is when both partners have the same Life Path number. For example, Tom might be learning how to develop a greater sense of other people's needs in his job as a sales rep. His wife, Jill, is working on developing the same sensitivities in her work as an attorney. In this respect, then, they are both working on the same Life Path *essence* but in different *kind*. They are experiencing similar lessons, perhaps even creating like-minded projects, but done separately from each other. When this happens, there is harmony in the relationship.

By comparing your chart with that of an intimate friend, look at the major positions on both charts. If one of you has the Life Path number and the other person has the same number for his or her Heart's Desire, the person with the Heart's Desire is drawn to the Life Path number because that person is doing in the world what their passion is calling for. Many people have so repressed their own heart's desires, they may have lost their remembrance of what fuels their passion. The individual with the Life Path is expressing that number pattern, whether they like it or not, and this expression calls to the person holding the Heart's Desire number.

Likewise, if the Essence number is the same as the Life Path number, the one holding the Essence number is attracted to the Life Path holder when he or she has denied her own Essence. In this instance, the Life Path holder is demonstrating out in the world what that number vibration calls for, a specific quality and expression of life, and it is this very quality of pattern which speaks to the heart of the Essence person. On the other hand, if the individual is able to clearly express his or her Essence, then the person who has the same

Life Path number is drawn to the Essence holder as a teacher and example.

When one person has a Power Goal number and is still fairly young, they will look to someone holding the Life Path number as a teacher to them because that person is already expressing what is in the younger person's future. Likewise, if the Power Goal person is in their Wisdom Cycle, the younger Life Path number person will look to the older person as a teacher for they have learned how to negotiate around the stumbling blocks of that particular pattern.

By adding together the Life Path numbers of you and your companion, you will find the single digit sum number of your shared path with all the challenges and creative potential associated with it. Refer to the sections in this book on the numbers, especially as expressed in the Life Path, and think in terms of two people, or a partnership working at that particular pattern. What would that look like? The following examples may offer clues:

Shared Life Paths

1

Your relationship will have a definite element of invention and exploring the unknown together. Allow your strength to be in a true partnership rather than being competitive towards each other.

2

As a couple you may be called upon to help others find new solutions for their conflicts or differences. You can create those bridges of understanding that help others (or yourself) to work in harmonious partnership with each other.

3

Your challenge is to find a way to be joyous together–to express your creativity, to be spontaneous, and to play. You can draw others into this delightful climate of playfulness.

4

You have come together to work and build something of substance that can withstand the rigors of time. You are challenged to persevere and be truthful to yourself and each other.

5

You have come together to experience the sensuality and adventure of the world. You could be great traveling companions, looking for thrills, visiting the Antarctic, climbing mountains, swimming with dolphins, promoting tours. And you'll enjoy sharing your adventures with friends. Promotion and salesmanship may be activities you could enjoy together.

6

Creating a home and family together would be a natural expression of a shared 6. Or perhaps you define your family in a broader way so that creating an environment of learning and healing for others would satisfy the 6 pattern. You could serve together in your community by volunteering to work at a shelter, feed the homeless, teach children, or being a patron of the arts. If your time and energy do not allow such ambitious plans, you will at least enjoy attending concerts and going to art shows as a couple.

7

The laboratory, sanctuary, library, university would be an environment to nurture your relationship. Or, if less formal, perhaps together you would want to study metaphysics and the psychic realms. The shared 7 indicates a relationship needing to search within for deeper wisdom.

8

As a team you could take on big projects involving other people. You could share leadership and raise large sums of money. Certainly, on a less ambitious scale, your having a shared 8 life path would indicate you are needing to organize your own finances so you can handle them with discrimination.

9

You could join a group such as the Peace Corps or a missionary service and together bring service and healing to others less fortunate than yourselves. You would want to reach beyond your personal relationship and allow your combined talents and skills to be a blessing to others.

As you consider your shared life path with your partner or beloved, take into the equation your personal life path and the qualities found in your name. If you are a personal 5 Life Path in a 7 Shared Life Path relationship, you might discover a tension between outward and inward needs. Remember the image of the bow and arrow---the taut string sends the arrow the farthest. Aim steady and true and let that tension create greatness between the two of you.

X

CONCLUSION

Y ou now have the fundamental information you need in this small book to faithfully interpret the Map of Numerology. Yet we have only covered the basics of an ancient system which has been added onto and reinterpreted many, many times over the centuries to accommodate the dramatic changes in science and civilization occurring since the days of Pythagorus. In the future, with the current research in the fields of physics and vibrational science, the study and significance of numerology may explode, revealing more and more about how it can help us understand and explain the human psyche.

As with all tools, mastery comes only with practice. In a study such as numerology, this mastery must include sharpening our intuition. Numbers are symbols for patterns; however, there are other symbolic languages that, together with numerology expand our appreciation for the wisdom and knowledge available to anyone who takes the time to learn the language of symbols. Consider the wisdom in the Tarot card for the Fool—that innocent willingness to step into the unknown, perhaps into danger, but with the joyous and free spirit of the child who trusts the universe. Or the significance of the planet Jupiter in our Astrology chart, indicating our area of profession. Likewise in Astrology, the tensions of squares or oppositions. These terms may mean nothing to you, but to an astrologer, they speak volumes.

Tools can be misused on occasion and too great a dependence upon them, to the neglect of your own inner wisdom and common sense, can be dangerous. When I first studied numerology I was fanatical about doing everyone's chart. During this time I remembered everyone's major position numbers and put them between me and my immediate experience of that person. One day a friend accused me of putting him in a box and said he didn't like that. Though I wanted to deny this at first, I realized he was right. I was putting everyone in the box of their numbers. This distorted my experience of them, keeping me from allowing them to change and reveal subtler levels of themselves. Since I was using the Western system of numerology at that time—which I've come to believe does not have the accuracy of the Chaldean system—I not only was misreading the chart, I was misreading the person as well. This was not using my common sense. Since then I hasten to immediately forget my clients' numbers.

I urge you to use the language of numerology to uplift the awareness and self esteem for whomever you do a chart by helping them to see the strength and contribution of their number patterns. What a world it would be if everyone were 6s or 8s! Can you imagine the power struggles that would go on? Every individual pattern is necessary for completing a whole that is much larger than any of us can even imagine.

When you do construct a chart for someone who is in pain or deep distress, help them to understand how a denial or negative expression of a number pattern may contribute to their pain. Show them the strengths present in their chart—which are always there—and the positive expressions of the problematic patterns. If they are open to this kind of help, guide them into developing affirmations to change their attitude, based on their number patterns.

We should always remember that we live in a world of vibration and have the power to change our reality through choice and consciousness. If we are sincere in our desire to evolve, becoming more compassionate in our relationships to ourselves and each other, we draw to ourselves the teachers and companions who take us by the hand, cheer our efforts and keep us from getting too far over our heads.

Use this map wisely. May it be a helpful guide through all your life experiences.

Blessings on your journey!

ADDENDUM
An example of a handwritten chart.
(Position names are given on page 54)

$$\frac{2}{} \quad \frac{6}{} \quad \frac{6}{} \quad = \quad 14/5$$

3/1 Linda Anne Walker

$$\frac{3 \; 54}{} \quad \frac{55}{} \quad \frac{6 \; 322}{}$$

$$\frac{12}{3} \quad \frac{10}{1} \quad \frac{13}{4} \quad = \quad 8$$

$$\frac{31541}{14/5} \quad \frac{1555}{16/7} \quad \frac{613252}{19/1} = 13 \quad = \quad 4$$

1 - 4	
2 - 2	
3 - 2	
4 - 1	
5 - 5	
6 - 1	
7 — 0	
8 — 0	

1-29   8
30-39 11/ 9
40-49 /PG 8
50-E   6

6
8
8   9
7 / 8
July 10, 1943 = 16/7
6   7
1
1

1999
1943
56 years

7
1
6
14/5 HLP

P = 6
E = 3
M = 4
I = 2

1997 = 16/7
98 = 8
99 = 9
2000 = 1

ABOUT THE AUTHOR...

Leeya Thompson has been a student of numerology for almost 40 years. She has enjoyed sharing her knowledge of this ancient map of consciousness through classes, hundreds of readings and now this book. She has a Masters Degree in Transpersonal Psychology giving her a broad background in the fields of Transpersonal psychology, spirituality and intuition. She draws upon these sources when offering a counseling session in numerology.

Leeya makes her home for part of the year in Northern California where she enjoys expressing her *3 Essence* in writing and playing with her three youngest grandchildren.

The Author and Morgan Faye, her youngest grandchild.

For information on readings or workshops, please contact:
Leeya Thompson
P.O. Box 994
Willits, CA 95490
E-mail: leeya@pacific.net

TENACITY PRESS

publishes books for expanding
self-knowledge and fostering
a closer relationship with the
Creative Consciousness from which
All is born.

Our books are available
in fine bookstores everywhere.

For more information
about our books,
lectures & workshops,
or the lectures, consulting,
workshops or personal
appearances
of any of our authors,
contact Susan at:

Phone: 1-800-738-6721
Fax: (707) 467-9159

E-mail us at: TenacityPR@aol.com